Endorsements

"I found Roberta Brown's book *A Mother's Wilderness Journey* very moving, as she honestly shared her experiences about the death of her beloved husband and then the enormous task she faced having to bring up their eight children. Anyone reading her book could understand the stresses and problems she had to face. I enjoyed her honest way of writing what she was going through, especially with the difficulties she faced with her rebellious daughter Sarah, who left home. Trusting in God to protect her, wherever she was, and to bring her safely back. I could relate to her story personally and was encouraged by it, because I was going through a similar situation with my own granddaughter who had also left our family and was mixing with the wrong people. As a Christian counsellor, with the OZ Challenge Inc ministry, and I work with people who have life controlling problems. I believe this book will greatly encourage parents who are going through a similar situation to trust in the Lord and know that He is in control. Roberta totally depended on her relationship with her Lord and Saviour Jesus Christ, and she saw many miracles, but also knew that she was in a spiritual battle for her daughter whom Satan had drawn into his dark kingdom (Eph 6:12). Roberta also had various Christian friends and prayer warriors who prayed and supported her throughout her ordeal. I highly recommend this book for parents who are going through a similar situation, for young people to understand the ordeal they are putting their family through when they leave home, and to be encouraged by this amazing testimony of the goodness of God."

Trudy Junginger, *Oz Challenge*

"Roberta Brown's book *'A Mother's Wilderness Journey'* is a deeply moving and honest account of a mother's unwavering faith through heartbreak and struggle. As she shares her journey of raising eight children after the loss of her husband - especially the painful challenges with her rebellious daughter - Roberta's story becomes a powerful source of encouragement for parents facing similar battles. Her trust in God, the power of prayer, and the support of a faith-filled community shine through every page. This book will bring hope to single parents and families dealing with addiction, reminding them that even in the darkest moments, God is at work."

Michael Foster, *Director of 'Answers in Genesis'*

A Mother's Wilderness Journey

THE BATTLE FOR MY DAUGHTER

ROBERTA BROWN

Ark House Press
arkhousepress.com

© 2025 Roberta Brown | deborahrising@outlook.com

All rights reserved. Apart from any fair dealing for the purpose of study, research, criticism, or review, as permitted under the Copyright Act, no part may be reproduced by any process without written permission.

Scriptures are taken from the New King James Version®. Copyright © 1982 by Thomas Nelson. Used by permission. All rights reserved.

Some names and identifying details have been changed to protect the privacy of individuals.

Cataloguing in Publication Data:
Title: A Mother's Wilderness Journey
ISBN: 978-1-7640298-9-6 (pbk)
Subjects: PSY038000   PSYCHOLOGY / Psychopathology / Addiction; REL099000 RELIGION / Christian Living / Spiritual Warfare; REL012160   RELIGION / Christian Living / Parenting;

Design by initiateagency.com

Dedication

I am dedicating my book to my family who I have been blessed with. My children, my grandchildren, my son and daughters-in-law who have been there through the years while I did my best to be the best parent I could be after my husband Philip died.

I also thank friends and those from my churches who were there for me when I went through times of struggle and needed prayer and support.

Thanks go to Oz Challenge who taught me much about Spiritual Warfare which helped me persevere in prayer.

Thanks also goes to Dr. Philip Jensen a Theologian at Cambridge who mentored me in the early stages of my writing journey.

Finally I dedicate this book to my Lord and Saviour Jesus Christ who never left my side through the journey and who promises to never leave me. Not only is he my Saviour and Lord, but has also been a husband to me during the often lonely wilderness journey of single parenthood and who helped me through the time of my daughters addiction.

Contents

Endorsements i
Dedication v
Introduction ix
Chapter 1:   The Awakening 1
Chapter 2:   The News 5
Chapter 3:   Off To Hospital 10
Chapter 4:   Last Days 14
Chapter 5:   No Saying Goodbye 17
Chapter 6:   Philip's Testimony 21
Chapter 7:   The Family Says Goodbye 27
Chapter 8:   Life Goes On 32
Chapter 9:   The Children 38
Chapter 10: God Watches Over Us And Miracles Do Happen ... 44
Chapter 11: My Two Eldest Girls Get Married 48
Chapter 12: Turmoil In The Camp 53
Chapter 13: A New Home, But Not For Long 57
Chapter 14: A New Home And A Torch Relay 64

Part Two

Chapter 15: Sarah 77
Chapter 16: Where To Get Help 82
Chapter 17: A Glimmer Of Hope 84
Chapter 18: Dark Days Ahead 87
Chapter 19: Learning How To Fight Back! 93

Chapter 20:	I Meet Tim	99
Chapter 21:	Realisation Dawns	103
Chapter 22:	The Strong Man	109
Chapter 23:	Weapons Of Our Warfare – Prayer	120
Chapter 24:	Weapons Of Our Warfare – The Word Of God	126
Chapter 25:	The Weapons Of Our Warfare – Praise	129
Chapter 26:	Weapons Of Our Warfare – Fellowship	131
Chapter 27:	Back To Bundaberg Again	134
Chapter 28:	My Other Children Bear My Load	139
Chapter 29:	God Keeps Her Safe	142
Chapter 30:	I Decide To Finally Take The Car Away!	147
Chapter 31:	Life Goes On, So Does The Fight	152
Chapter 32:	Sharing The Load	156
Chapter 33:	The Car Is Gone Again!	159
Chapter 34:	I Learn An Important Lesson	162
Chapter 35:	Home At Last	165
Chapter 36:	A Movie, A Man Of God, And An Ex-drug Addict	169
Chapter 37:	A Challenge For 'Teen Challenge'	173
Chapter 38:	A Beautiful Graduation And A Huge Disappointment	178
Chapter 39:	Mercy And A God Of Second Chances	183
Chapter 40:	Mercy At Last	188
Chapter 41:	A Baby Called Grace	191
Chapter 42:	Dancing Again	196
Chapter 43:	Tim	198
Chapter 44:	A Rainbow And Two Weddings	200
Chapter 45:	Two New Grandsons And A Flood!	207
Chapter 46:	A Dance School Is Born	211
Chapter 47:	A Dance School Flourishes	214
Chapter 48:	God's Goodness Astounds Me!	216

Introduction

Do not remember the former things,
Nor consider the things of old.
Behold, I will do a new thing,
Now it shall spring forth;
Shall you not know it?
I will even make a road in the wilderness
And rivers in the desert.
(Isa.43:18-19)

This is a story I never imagined I would write. As a mother who, along with her husband, did our best to bring up our children to follow Christ, we never contemplated the possibility that one of our precious children would become a drug addict!

In fact you could say it is a parent's worst nightmare. Christian or not, we all love our children, and desire to give them the very best upbringing we can but, of course the enemy of our souls wants nothing but destruction and death. I would like to say that the Christian life is always wonderful, but I am reminded that, *"…in the world you will have tribulation…"* (John 16:33)

Every one of us will go through times of trial, and it is no different for Christians. It is how we deal with those moments in life. Do we turn and blame God and retreat into our shells, or do we allow God to use these times to grow our faith and believe Romans 8:35 which says: *"Who shall separate us from the love of Christ? Shall tribulation, or famine, or nakedness, or peril, or sword?"* Then in verse 37 we read: *"Yet we are more than conquerors through Him who loved us".*

My story is one of heartache, struggles, consuming prayer, and ultimate victory through Christ. Parents, grandparents, and friends of those suffering dreadful addiction and dependency on drugs, need to know that there is hope. It is about standing on the promises of God in dealing with teenagers and young adults who rebel, and may reject the Christian life.

My story is also about bringing up a big family as a single parent, and dealing with multiple personalities, financial struggles, and dealing with all the changes that happen when two become one, and all the difficult decisions are yours alone to make!

I believe God prepares us to face the larger trials of life by bringing us through the smaller valleys we face each day. I hope you will cry in times of despair, with me, and also rejoice in victory as the Lord does his job of restoration!

Chapter 1

THE AWAKENING

It was a warm beautiful day in the autumn of 2004, when I rose early to begin a day shift at a nearby hospital. I gazed out of the window of the home we rented to the bush, which was full of vibrant colours of green from tropical plants, to the violets and pinks of the bush orchids. I loved this little house which wasn't fancy, hidden away in the Australian bush, but still close to the school and shops.

I had the four children still at home. The eldest was Sarah, who was in Year 11 at high school, and her sister Leah who was in Year 9. Then there were the twins, Joe and Ben, who were in their final year at the primary school opposite our home. I left them to get their breakfast, and get themselves ready for school, as I began the 30-minute drive to the hospital and, as I drove I prayed, as I did almost every time I was in the car, for a good day at work and that the Lord would look after my family.

I arrived on the busy medical ward, and listened to the night staff hand over the patient's information from the night shift. I was the nurse assigned to a young teenage girl who was recovering from a drug overdose. Her parents were distraught, and I remember thinking, 'I'm glad I don't have to deal with a suicidal teenager!' If only I had known, in that minute, what was ahead of me, for very soon I would be confronted with a brutal reality.

It was a sombre morning on the ward, and we soon found out the reason why when all the staff were called into the office. We looked at each other with puzzlement, as it was out of the ordinary for everyone to be called to the nurse manager's office at once! It was then that we learned the heartbreaking news that one of our fellow nurses, who had been in hospital, had just had her life support turned off.

It was such a shock, as I had worked with this amazing nurse a week before, and she had shown no signs of being ill. This nurse was from my town in the Sunshine Coast hinterland of Queensland, and was a quiet hard-working nurse, who never complained and never had a bad word to say about anyone. She loved to go line dancing, and was on the local swim club committee. A week before she began to have chest pains, and suffered a heart attack. It was necessary for her to be transported to the Royal Brisbane intensive care unit, where she was put on life support. It turned out that she had cancer, and had no idea until it was too much for her heart!

All of the staff were devastated and as we tried to deal with this dreadful news, I was told there was a phone call for me at the front desk.

"Hello. It's Roberta Brown here. Can I help you?"

"Roberta, it's the sports teacher from the high school, I have some bad news about your daughter, Sarah. She was seen taking some pills, and luckily her friend came and told me about it immediately when he saw what she was doing. Sarah seems to be alright, and is here with me. I think you need to come straight away!"

I was shocked and bewildered, and taken completely by surprise, not even able to think clearly and instruct the teacher to get an ambulance! In shock I told my Nurse Manager that I had an emergency at the school, and had to go and see my daughter. I hurried to my car and drove, in disbelief, with a huge knot in the pit of my stomach.

Sarah was an incredibly gifted student, with everything going for her. She was smart, athletic, and played the flute in the school band. What reason could she have for taking pain killers? As soon as I arrived the teacher met me and took me to her office, and there was Sarah looking downcast and staring at the floor. I sat there, numb, while I was told about all the struggles my daughter was having. My thoughts were half with what the teacher was saying, and half wondering why we were still sitting here discussing my daughter when she should have been in the hospital!

I can't remember much of that conversation, but I finally told the teacher that I had to get my daughter to the hospital, and walked with Sarah through the school grounds with everyone's eyes on us. In the car I tried to keep calm while I asked her what she had taken.

"Just some pain medication, Mum," she replied looking down at her feet.

Paracetamol is a great pain reliever if used correctly and, while it is very common and may seem harmless, if too much is ingested at once it can cause irreparable liver damage. I berated myself, and the school, for not calling an ambulance!

"Why would you take so many pain killers, Sarah?"

"I don't know, Mum. To stop feeling bad I guess."

"What could be so bad that you would want to harm yourself?" I asked.

As soon as we were at Emergency, they ushered us into a cubicle, and the doctor again asked Sarah what she had taken. The hospital staff quickly set her up with an infusion to counteract any effects the medication may have had on the liver.

The only thing I remember that day was the awkwardness and confusion I felt as I tried to grapple with the fact that my daughter could feel so bad about herself as to take pills to stop her emotional pain. How could I not have noticed what was happening? I sat there watching the drip, drip of the infusion, thankful that it wasn't more serious, and it wasn't sedatives or hard drugs that she had taken!

Once she was medically cleared for discharge, a woman from the mental health unit came and interviewed her. This lady looked friendly, and smiled at us as if there was nothing in the world to worry about. I was not allowed to accompany my daughter into the interview room, even though it was clear that I was her mother, and in a nurse's uniform! Whatever was said, the mental health worker seemed convinced that she would be unlikely to overdose again. No follow up was done, and no further help was offered. I thought that at least a few days in the mental health ward would help. It was as if nothing had happened and, as a parent, I felt totally helpless to deal with the situation!

The drive home didn't seem real, and I didn't know what to say to my beautiful daughter who was only fifteen and was obviously struggling with depression. I couldn't sleep, tossing and turning as I thought over what had transpired that day. Before I fell to sleep exhausted, I cried out to God!

"Please, God, let this be the one and only time this happens. Have I done something to cause this, and how can I support my daughter?"

This was not the last time Sarah would take an overdose, and the rough road was to continue for the next five years!

Chapter 2

THE NEWS

The problems really began back in the year 1999, which was the year my husband had to grapple with the news that he had a brain tumour. It was discovered by accident on a routine eye exam which alerted the optometrist, leading to my husband having a CT scan. It was a benign tumour and, according to the neurosurgeon, it would have been growing there slowly for the last several years.

It should have been a pleasant drive, but was one of trepidation as we silently drove down the M1 towards Brisbane. This was the day when we would speak to the neurosurgeon concerning what could be done about Philip's brain tumour. We met him in his private office near the Roma Street parklands. It was a beautiful day, but it made no difference to the horrible feeling I had in the pit of my stomach! My husband and I were shown into the neurosurgeon's office as he introduced himself.

"Hello, Mr and Mrs Brown. I am the surgeon assigned to your case. Won't you sit down? I imagine you are both concerned about the tumour we found, and I would like to discuss what sort of growth it is, and what can be done about it. This particular tumour is benign, which means it is not able to spread to other areas of the body. It is known as a Craniopharingioma, and the main concern with this type is how it is encroaching on the optic nerve which affects sight and also on the Pituitary gland which can affect hormone production."

He was very calm as he had probably discussed this very thing with hundreds of patients before us. There was little emotion or empathy displayed, which should have put us at ease. But didn't.

"Does this mean that his eyesight will get worse?" I asked.

The surgeon replied, "Yes, I'm afraid it will make his eyesight deteriorate if left alone."

This was devastating news as my husband, Phil, was an avid reader who loved his books and his Bible. The fact that the pituitary gland would also be affected meant all other glands and their function would be compromised.

The surgeon went on to say, "It's a slow growing tumour, and will not spread to other areas. I feel the best decision is to leave things as they are, and see what happens in the future. I would not worry too much and, meanwhile, you will go on the list for surgery, if that is the way you both choose to go."

There was no other treatment offered and, as I look back, I wonder why there was no suggestion of radiation therapy, or any alternative? Phil and I left the specialist's rooms, not feeling any more relieved than when we arrived. My husband was a very positive person, and appeared calm as we drove home, while I wondered what the future held?

My husband and I had eight children. They were ages seven to 20, and six of the children still lived at home. My two eldest daughters, Naomi and Esther, were studying for their degrees at universities in Brisbane, while the younger children were still at schools in Beerwah. My husband was seventeen years older than me, but still a reasonably young man at 61.

THE NEWS

Soon after we had the news about his brain tumour, Philip graduated from university with a Bachelor of Arts degree. It was a bitter sweet moment, as he had worked so hard to complete his degree, spending hours on the computer and at university. It should have been a special day for Philip to go up on the stage, with his family watching, to receive his degree, but he looked older than his 61 years and, I believe, since the news of his brain tumour, he had lost his zest for living.

I often look back before this time and feel that, in a way, studying for his degree had actually robbed his family of what would be his last few years with us. He would leave early in the morning, and not arrive home until very late at night. There were days when we hardly ever saw him. Of course, none of us knew what was ahead. It makes you realise how short life is, and how precious are the moments we have together. We need to treat every day as a precious gift from God.

It wasn't long before Philips condition deteriorated, with increasing concern over his eye-sight, which was getting worse, especially his peripheral vision as he still insisted on driving. A month before he went into hospital for surgery, Sarah, and her sister Leah, were performing in the Sunshine Coast Singfest Extravaganza. It took students from many Sunshine Coast primary schools, and formed them into one choir under a famous conductor. For weeks they would practise songs together.

The time came for them to perform at the Church's hall at Woombye. There was a particular song which required a flute solo, and Sarah played the flute with her school band. Although another girl had the part, Sarah's music teacher asked for Sarah to join in doing a duet. The song is about a sparrow which falls to the ground, but another young sparrow replaces the dying sparrow. It is a very sad song called 'Take these wings', by the composer Don Besig. The flutes and singing are beautiful to listen to.

Playing the CD from that night brings back so many memories, and reminds me of the fact that Philip's life would soon be over like the sparrow in the song, as it was almost exactly one month later I would say goodbye to my dear husband for good. The song is also a reminder that our lives don't end in this life but, unlike the sparrow, our lives will be everlasting if we are in Christ. We are precious to God and the Bible says: *"And do not fear those who kill the body but cannot kill the soul. But rather fear him who is able to destroy both soul and body in Hell. Are not two sparrows sold for a copper coin? And not one of them falls to the ground apart from your Father's will."* (Matthew 10: 28-29)

I was very proud of my daughters, Sarah and Leah, as they sang, and Sarah played her flute. It was a very memorable night. As we left the hall, my husband got in the van before me and insisted on driving home. We were driving down the dual carriageway with Phil, myself, Sarah, Leah, and the twins, Joe and Ben, in our green van, when I began to notice the van was drifting into the next lane, making me increasingly nervous. I kept a close eye on the situation, but it was the final straw when my husband missed our turnoff to Beerwah.

"Phil, you need to pull over and let me drive as I don't think you can see properly and it's putting your family's life in danger!"

I felt terrible that I had to take the keys off him, especially in front of the children. The look on his face was devastating, but he didn't argue, and handed over the keys with resignation. I was also concerned about his general health, as he was becoming increasingly tired, needing to lie down through the day. He had also lost his appetite. I later realised these were both signs that his hormones were imbalanced, and the tumour was affecting his Pituitary function.

One day, when he was lying down on the bed in our room, he said, "Robbie, do you see that man there. He's been talking to me."

THE NEWS

"Where Phil?"

"Over by the TV."

Of course, there was no one there, and it turned out to be an actor on the TV show he had been watching. He believed the man was in the room, speaking to him. This triggered further alarm bells, and many times he would say things that made no sense to me. He was so confused that he didn't think he needed to see a doctor. In the doctor's surgery, he thought we were there because there was something wrong with me!

He said, "Doctor, I think my wife needs testosterone."

The doctor could see how confused he was, and ordered a brain CT. It showed he had an accumulation of fluid, known as hydrocephalus, which meant he would need to be admitted to hospital.

Chapter 3

OFF TO HOSPITAL

The hospital which specialised in neurology was the Royal Brisbane, which is one of the largest hospitals in Queensland. My family and I lived on the Sunshine Coast, which was an hour away. As soon as he was admitted, the endocrine specialist looked at his hormone levels to sort out the imbalance, and gave him hormone replacements. While he was in the Royal, the surgeon and other doctors discussed whether or not surgery was an option.

Phil remained slightly confused and, early one night, I received a call from the hospital to say that my husband was missing!

"What do you mean my husband is missing? Where would he go in the middle of the night in Brisbane wearing pyjamas?"

"Mrs Brown, we know he had a visitor, and we believe he may have walked out of the hospital with this person."

I was incredulous! How could they lose a grown man? The story emerged that a friend of my eldest daughter visited my husband in hospital. Philip was always very chatty and, as they talked, the young man in question allowed my husband, in his dressing gown, to accompany him out of the ward. Instead of Philip turning around and going back into the hospital, he decided to take a walk in his confused state.

"Please Lord, find my husband and bring him safely back to the hospital, and keep him safe," I cried.

Down the road from the hospital is an area of Brisbane known as the 'Valley'. It is a favourite nightspot, with many clubs, restaurants, and bars. There is also a major Brisbane rail station close by. My husband was familiar with the area, and would stop for coffee or breakfast on the way to university where he had studied for his degree. It reminded me of the times we would take the children into the city on the train, and go to the big McWhirters Marketplace shopping mall in Brunswick Street. We would have McDonald's for breakfast, and browse around the quirky shops in the mall, before boarding the train again to go into central Brisbane.

Having a neurological condition, with signs of confusion, it was considered important enough for the police to help find him.

It was a Friday night, and I lay beside the phone waiting for that all important word from the hospital. I was exhausted with worry, and had fallen asleep, when I woke suddenly to hear the phone ringing. I was expecting it would be the hospital, or the police, on the line to tell me they had found Phil, but was shocked to hear my husband's voice instead!

"Hi Robbie, it's Phil. I'm at the train station at Brunswick Street. I've bought a ticket to come home to Beerwah, and should be at the Beerwah station about 11 o'clock."

This was what he would say if he was coming home from university and was wanting me to pick him up from the station. Philip had automatically made his way to the station where he had gone many, many times before, an automatic response to find his way home! I was wondering how he got there, and how he could possibly have a ticket to Beerwah at this time of night? He sounded so normal, and was doing something that he had always done, buy a ticket home and ask me to meet him at the station. In hindsight I wish I had let him do just that and leave Brisbane, board the train, and come home to his family, like he always had. He was never to have that opportunity again!

I needed to get my husband back to the hospital safely, so I calmly spoke to him saying, "Phil the police are out looking for you, and they need you to go back to hospital because of your condition. You have to go to the mall near the station, and tell the police officer stationed there that you are the man from the Royal Brisbane Hospital who they are looking for."

I was thankful Phil had decided to phone me, and let me know where he was. He agreed to find the police, and let them know he was the one they were looking for. I hung up the phone, praying he would follow my instructions and, 30 minutes later, the hospital rang to say he was safely back.

"Thank you, God, for watching over my husband and getting him back to hospital safely," I cried!

When my husband had passed away, I collected his belongings from the hospital and found a train ticket in his dressing gown pocket, along with a ticket to the movie, 'The Green Mile' with Tom Hanks, dated the same day, the day he escaped from the hospital!

After a few days of hormone replacement, my husband became much more like himself. Phil was a talker and loved people. He would chat to patients and staff, and to any visitors who would walk in.

One day he said to me, "Robbie there is a lady here who is suffering from terrible back pain, and I told her that you would pray for her."

I had travelled over an hour to visit my husband, but he was more concerned about the lady with the back pain. I did as I was asked, introduced myself, and was able to pray with her.

OFF TO HOSPITAL

Another time while travelling to the hospital, I noticed a tyre was flat on the van. My son, Aaron, was sixteen at the time, and he encouraged me to drive over the overpass to the service centre on the other side. I wondered how we were going to manage to change the tyre on our green van, and still make it in time to the hospital for visiting hours. I asked God to please send someone to help us and, no sooner had we parked at the service station, than a young man approached us and offered to help with our tyre change. God always sends his angel just in time! It took no time to get back on the road to Brisbane.

The reason this day was important to us was because it was our youngest daughter Leah's tenth birthday, and I had bought a cake to share with Phil. When I arrived at the hospital with my six children, the staff were kind enough to supply bowls, cups, and a room where we could go and celebrate together. It wasn't long enough, the time we had was brief but, of course, you live in the moment not knowing what is ahead of you. The difficulties were many, from having to find money for petrol and parking, to trying to juggle the children's schooling and activities with the trips to hospital. Somehow we managed, with God's help, and the kindness of my church who supplied meals for us at this busy time.

Chapter 4

LAST DAYS

The surgeon spoke to Phil and I about having surgery to remove as much of the tumour as possible. The surgeon believed it was the best solution, considering my husband's eyesight was failing, and the problems he had with his hormone function. I do not remember being given any alternatives to the surgery, and it was a decision I later regretted we had made because of the possible complications which could occur. I knew that it was possible for my husband to survive the surgery, as my father had a similar tumour removed and lived a further 39 years. My father lived a normal life with all his hormone function being managed with medication. Believing it was in Philip's best interest, we decided to go ahead.

The day of the surgery arrived, and I was too late to see Phil as he was already in theatre. I did get the chance of having a hug the day before, and praying with him. He seemed in good spirits. My husband was forever the optimist, and left all the worry to me! A close family friend offered to spend the day with me, and we prayed and drank coffee, ate lunch, and just waited and waited for news. Many people, including friends and family, were praying for him. I don't know how I managed to get through that time, and I am grateful to my beautiful friend Judy for her company.

Finally we received the news that he was out of surgery and in the intensive care unit, where he would stay for a few days of recovery. I was an official with Little Athletics at Glasshouse Mountains. Six of my children were involved, and there was a coaching course being run at the nearby University of Queensland athletics track. I had enrolled some months before, and the club paid for my two night's accommodation in Brisbane. This was a provision of God that I could stay, free of charge, in a hotel close by the hospital.

I shared a room with a friend, Vickie, and through the day I trained at the nearby University track, and visited the hospital after to check on my husband. He mainly slept through the first few days. I had my phone with me all the time in case there were any changes to his condition. I just stayed by his bed in intensive care, as there was little I could do but pray. My two eldest daughters, Naomi and Esther who were at university, were also able to visit him.

After a few days my husband was transferred to the ward. He had been walking and talking normally before the surgery but, since the surgery, he had suffered a stroke, with weakness down his right side. Twice he fell. Once in the shower, and once when a young doctor asked him to follow his finger as he tested his eyesight. He followed it until he overbalanced and fell off his chair! He could talk but, when I would visit, he was often in bed asleep. It didn't help that the area around his bed had very little room, as this part of the hospital was very old.

Most days I was busy at home with the children and school. The last day I saw my husband it was a Friday and, when I went to see him, he was sleeping in bed again. I waited and waited to see if he would wake up before I went, but he didn't. I am comforted to know that he had other visitors when I was unable to see him. The pastor from the Baptist church visited him and Phil, in his friendly fashion, would get people to go to the canteen and get him food. A few of my daughter's friends would come in too as they lived in Brisbane.

Feelings of guilt would often make me angry that I didn't make more of an effort to wake him on those occasions. I never got to see him, or talk to him, before he died. There was no way of knowing that he was going to die in the next few days, but this didn't make it any easier to accept the terrible news when it came! The medical staff were discussing his rehabilitation! He was getting ready to be transferred to the Sunshine Coast the following week, which meant the family could see him more often. I was so looking forward to not having to travel all the way to Brisbane, as it was taking its toll on me and on our finances.

Chapter 5

NO SAYING GOODBYE

I was at home on Sunday night and a thought crossed my mind that I should phone the hospital to talk to Phil. However, on reflection, I thought that I'd see him Tuesday, and he would probably be sleeping anyway. I have learned to pay attention to thoughts that often appear fleeting, as it is often the Lord speaking to us. I was planning to talk to the social worker on the Tuesday at the hospital, to discuss transport to his radiotherapy appointments.

Someone who did ring the hospital was Phil's sister in Canada. Maureen lived on Vancouver Island where Philip was born, and she was able to talk to her brother a few days before he died. Phil's older brother, Mel, died of cancer some years before.

Monday was a strange day, and it was a day of preparation which, I believe, God orchestrated. I was down at the Beerwah shops, and saw two friends sitting on a bench. Both were widows, and I asked, "What have you ladies been doing today?"

They told me they had been down to the Beerwah cemetery to see their husband's graves. One of the husbands buried there was known to Phil, and he used to spend time discussing the Bible and their differing beliefs. The other had been the husband of my dear friend, Flo, who used to arrange the flowers at the Baptist church.

After talking to my two friends, I drove my eldest son to Caloundra for an x-ray, and was looking at the second-hand shops. I found a nice pair of cream-coloured pants and a black top, which went well together. It was the black top I would wear at my husband's funeral!

I belonged to the Baptist church at this time, and the church ladies had kindly arranged for different people to bring an evening meal, as I was busy with travelling in and out of Brisbane. Just before my friend, Heather, dropped off some pizzas, I had a call from the hospital to say my husband had a turn, and I should come straight in. With a quick explanation to the children, I jumped in the van with trepidation. It was the longest drive of my life. I left My 16-year-old son, Aaron, with the younger children, and quickly alerted my parents and two eldest daughters to meet me at the hospital. I was frustrated as I circled the carpark looking for parking, wondering how Phil was.

"Please, God. Let him be alright," I silently prayed.

I went straight to the ward, but my husband wasn't there and they asked me to wait in a small room in the intensive care unit. As I sat there, a feeling of foreboding came over me which seemed like a weight on my shoulders, and I felt the room begin to spin as I came to the realisation that my husband had possibly passed away! It was the longest few minutes of my life!

A doctor came and said, "I am sorry, but your husband had a blood clot that travelled to the lung. We attempted CPR for over an hour, but we couldn't bring him back."

In stunned silence I followed him, as in a dream, to a curtained off bed, and saw my dear husband, Phil, lying peacefully as if he was sleeping. I sat there holding his hand, thinking he looked better than I had ever seen him. The bandages were gone from the operation site, and there was little evidence of scaring. He was at peace, and I knew he was with Jesus, but I couldn't understand why God would take him so soon and leave me alone with eight children!

As I sat there I forgot that the rest of the family were coming, and they didn't yet know the worst. Before I could go and call anyone, the nurse, not realising that the other family members were unaware he had died, ushered my daughter, Esther, into the room. The shock she must have felt was terrible, and the nurse should have waited until I could speak to the family. We hugged and, as Esther sat beside her father, I went quickly to the corridor where my parents, and other daughter, Naomi, were waiting. As I went to hug my father, the realisation of what had happened hit me, and I felt my knees suddenly give way. Sobbing, I fell into his arms.

At home the other children were asleep. It seems, when we look back on times like these, we wonder why we do the things we do? There are so many conflicting emotions going through our minds at the time. I decided to ring my eldest son, Aaron, and tell him about his father. Because he was 16, I felt he had the right to know what was happening at the hospital.

"Aaron," I said. "I'm at the hospital, and I have some very sad news. Your dad had some complications, and a clot went to his lungs. They couldn't save him, son. He passed away. I'm so sorry to have to tell you this, Aaron. I felt you had a right to know. If you could please not tell the younger children, I will share with them in the morning. I will be home later with your sister, Esther."

I never thought about him being alone, and how he would take it. Later, my daughter Leah, would tell me that she heard him crying and, when she asked him why, he made excuses about it having to do with his athletics. I didn't want any of the other children told until I came home in the morning. He must have been devastated by the news! I have since told him how sorry I was that he had to deal with the news of his father's death alone.

My daughter, Esther, decided to come home with me and stay, as I didn't feel like driving home by myself. How I managed to drive home is something I must have done on auto-pilot, as my mind was wondering how I would tell the children about their father! At breakfast I gathered all the family together to give them the news about their dad. It was one of the hardest things I have ever had to do.

I walked into the room feeling drained and uneasy. To face those young people with the news, was heart wrenching. All my children turned to look at me as I sat at the table.

"I am so very sorry to tell you this, kids, but your father won't be coming home. He has gone to be with Jesus! It was sudden, and they couldn't save him, although the doctors and nurses worked hard to bring him back. A clot blocked the main artery, and stopped his heart from working."

There was silence, as each child tried to take in the news. The twins, Joe and Ben, were only seven years old, their sister, Leah, 10 and Sarah, 11. The older boys, Jacob and Aaron, were 13 and 16. This was the turning point for my daughter, Sarah, and it is a moment she would not forget. It wasn't as if the other children were not affected, because each of them suffered loss but, to different degrees and in different ways.

However, for Sarah at just 11 years old, it was a trauma that would affect her young spirit for years to come. Approaching puberty and early teenage years without her father, and having a perfectionist, striving personality, it became more and more difficult for her to cope with life.

Chapter 6

PHILIP'S TESTIMONY

My biggest regret was being unable to say goodbye to my husband. One minute we were preparing for him to be transferred to another hospital, and the next he had passed away! So many people had been praying for him when he first went into hospital, and as he came through the surgery. I think we then become complacent, and stop praying with the same intensity. I often wonder if he didn't somehow know that he would not be coming home.

Before he had his surgery he would talk about the children and what they should do with their lives. He said to me one day, "Robbie, I've been talking to the nursing staff, and you know the money isn't too bad. You should go back to nursing again."

Can you imagine me working as a nurse, looking after my big family, and having to look after my husband post-surgery!

Another time he said, "Rob you need to find out about this First Home Owner Grant."

Before we were married, Phil had owned a few rental properties and so I wondered why he would suggest I find out about the First Home Owner Grant. He wasn't eligible, and I would only be eligible if he was not here!

He loved the Lord, and had become a Christian later in life. His father had never given up praying for him. He was the black sheep of the family, and was the youngest of three children, with his siblings, Mel and Joan, being 10 years or more older then Philip. His mother and father owned businesses, which meant they were not around much, and the young Phil was left on his own a lot.

He was very enterprising growing up, and had all sorts of ways to make money on the side. He grew up in Canada and, in one place they lived, it was very inaccessible, where his parents ran a hotel. The only way you could get in and out was by boat. He used to collect all the beer bottles, and get money for them. No doubt he got to know all the characters off the boats. He had a very outgoing personality, and could charm anyone!

I met my husband in Western Australia, where he owned a pool company and I was a nurse. I actually met him in a nightclub and, I thought to myself when I saw him on the dance floor, 'Good grief. He thinks he's Peter Allen!' Peter Allen was a very flamboyant Aussie entertainer, and would dance, sing, and play the piano. Later on, Hugh Jackman would play the part in the musical 'The Boy from Oz'.

It's also interesting that I had been brought up in Vancouver B.C. on the west coast of Canada. We moved back to Scotland when I was 13. Phil had been born in the city of Victoria, on Vancouver Island, just off the coast from Vancouver. In a way we had a few similarities in our upbringing, but it would be eight years after leaving Canada that I would eventually meet my husband in Perth, Western Australia.

It was on a trip back to Canada, before we were married, that the Lord would speak to my husband and I. We spent a lot of time on that trip, travelling up and down the length and breadth of British Colombia. We even travelled around Vancouver Island, where I met his sister and her husband. We also went to Alberta, where it snowed, even in April!

Often we would be listening to the radio, and there was always a preacher talking about salvation, and getting our lives right with God. It was strange that we would listen to the radio in silence, not realising that, slowly, God was working in us both. There were a few adventures on that trip, and you have to appreciate the beauty of Canada, especially the Rocky Mountains, and places like Banff and Lake Louise, with the pristine lakes and rugged, snow-covered mountains.

We would drive through acres of pine forests, drive over winding hilly motorways and, one night, we even visited a rubbish tip to watch the black bears eat their fill of leftovers! Phil and I even tried our hand at salmon fishing, with very little success! Then we would watch the native Canadian Indians carry their catches on large poles, where there would be half a dozen large salmon strung up. The native Indians were allowed to gaff the salmon on their way up stream, but the rest of us had to use fishing lines.

Phil had been going on sales trips around the province, though often these were not successful and we would be very short of money. It was Christmas, and we were holed up in a motel in a town called Prince George, basically snowed in with no money and little food. A few days before Christmas, Phil's father, Freeman, sent a hundred dollars by bank transfer, and the only catch was we were snowed in with no petrol, so Phil had to hike into town in the snow so we could get the money to buy groceries! I do think the Lord was definitely trying to get through to us in those days.

We both decided that the situation wasn't good and that I should fly home to Western Australia, as I wasn't able to work in Canada. Phil would come to join me once he had the money. Meanwhile, I found out I was pregnant with our first child, so we returned to Vancouver and, with a few of my Canadian relatives as witnesses, we were married in a registry office in New Westminster. By this time, we both had decided to return to our Christian roots.

A church wedding would have been lovely but, under the circumstances, we felt it wasn't to be. Instead we asked the Lord to be with us in that small registry office in New Westminster, Canada and, soon after with money sent to me by my parents, I was on a plane, flying alone back to Perth! I lived with my parents while waiting for Phil to return to Australia. He had been an Australian resident, but had no re-entry visa. It was up to me to find all the documentation and proof of his Australian residency, before they would let Philip back into the country! It was a trying time as I was preparing for the arrival of our first child.

Eventually the day came when my husband returned to Australia, and I was able to meet him at Perth airport. It was a very changed man that I met at that airport. He had grown spiritually, and was a different person in that God had begun to do a mighty work in him!

Through Christ, he had given up on striving to make lots of money and simply living for himself. He was able to eventually stop smoking, and give up alcohol. It wasn't an overnight thing but, with a few nudges from myself and a desire to do the right thing by our beautiful baby daughter, Naomi, he was able to exceedingly abundantly, with God's help, stop the addictive behaviours, and focus on bringing up his family. He was an alcoholic, and could never touch it again without it taking hold of him.

In the 21 years of our marriage, he only fell off the wagon once, and that was while selling land in Darwin for a developer in Cairns. We lived in Cairns, North Queensland, and Phil would follow up the leads that came into the office. He was away in Darwin for about a week, and I had just found out I was pregnant for the fourth time and was very excited. I felt really well with no morning sickness, which was unusual for me. A few days before Phil was meant to come home, there was a phone call from him explaining he had had a car accident and was in hospital with a damaged knee. My husband offered very little information, except that it would be a few days before he could get home.

Just before he arrived back from his trip, I began to experience blood loss and realised I was having a miscarriage. I was devastated at the news, later concluding that the reason I had no morning sickness was because the pregnancy had never been properly established.

When Phil arrived at the airport, I had to tell him I thought I was having a miscarriage, but this wasn't the only bad news! He came off the plane limping with a walking stick, and then told me the reason he had the accident was because he had started drinking again.

One has to appreciate the drinking culture in Australia, especially in Darwin where the weather is tropical, hot with high humidity, and nearly the whole population drinks, especially beer. My husband would get around this when going on his sales calls by saying, when he was offered a beer, "No thanks, but I'd love a cup of tea."

This worked well until he came to a house where the canny owner, figuring that Phil was driving and didn't want to go over the limit, offered him a light beer instead of tea. It was at that point the temptation became too much, and my husband relented and accepted the drink. From then on he would drink light beer until, at one house, they had none and he was then on full strength. How quickly can we fall from Grace. From drinking tea, to being out of control were only a few steps away.

The Bible reminds us in 1 Peter 5:8, *"Be sober, be vigilant; because the Devil walks about like a roaring lion, seeking whom he may devour."*

I believe the Devil targets our weaknesses, so we need to know our own natures, and daily put on the armour of God. Phil found himself standing at the bar of the hotel, drinking, and realised that he had succumbed to temptation and was now out of control! He cried out to God in his heart to please stop him from continuing to drink. He then got in the rental car and drove towards Katherine Gorge where he had an accident which could have taken his life!

God did not let him perish, but had mercy and, though he could have died, only his knee was damaged in the accident. He should have been prosecuted for a drink driving offence, but got off on a technicality because of a mistake by the police. I was devastated at the news when he arrived back in Cairns, but he was alive and never again did he allow another drop of alcohol to pass his lips!

Chapter 7

THE FAMILY SAYS GOODBYE

The time came to organise my husband's funeral. I never knew how hard this would be until faced with all the small decisions I had to make. Grief is hard enough, but having to think about what casket, whether the coffin would be open or closed, and who would do the service, was stressful to contemplate. My husband hadn't worked for a few months, and hadn't kept up the insurance payments through work, so there was no money! A funeral home in Nambour had his body, and were preparing it for burial, but to have them do a proper service would cost thousands.

Everything seemed very unreal after Phil died, and I would wander around the house in a daze. I had friends who were a lovely couple, and had attended our church. David ran a funeral home, and his wife helped him part-time. I rang him to get some much-needed advice.

"David, I have some sad news. My husband, Philip, has passed away and I have to think about his funeral. I don't know what to do as I have never had to organise a funeral before!"

"Roberta, I am so sorry to hear this, and I am happy to come over and talk about what would be the best to do in your circumstances."

As I spoke to David, the tears silently ran down my cheeks. I made an effort to not sob openly, as David said he was happy to come over and speak to me. The next day David arrived and spoke to me about my circumstances.

"Roberta, a funeral is very expensive and, with no funeral insurance or Super, it's not really a good option to have a traditional funeral," David reminded me.

"David, I want to give my husband a good send off, and make it special. My children are saying goodbye to their dad!"

"Roberta, you have a large family with no money coming in. You and the children are what's important now, and Philip would've agreed! Can I suggest a compromise. Have a memorial service for the public and friends, where there's no coffin, but a table arranged with special photos of Phil and the family. Have a short graveside service with close family and the pastor after the memorial. Allow the state to supply the coffin, which will cost you nothing! You and the children are more important than a fancy coffin."

So, instead of a big funeral, I decided on a memorial service in the Baptist church, and a private funeral service at the graveside. I was so grateful to David for his input, which made all the decisions I had to make much easier.

The day of the memorial service came, and it was a glorious winters day. The Sun shone, and the sky was so blue, it reminded me of Phil's eyes which were a piercing blue and were always crinkled up when he was joking around. He could see the funny side of everything! He was working as a security guard and sometimes he had the exciting job of guarding a bank! Standing outside a bank all day, watching people come in and out, would seem like the most boring of jobs, but not for Phil. He would come home from work and have the children and I in stitches over the stories of people he would encounter. He was friendly, and would hold open the door for the elderly, and say hello to everyone. What made him laugh most was the frantic attempts people would make to remember their pin numbers! They would type one in after the other until, out of frustration, they would finally give up and actually go into the bank!

My lovely friends, David and Kristina, who owned the funeral business came to the memorial service, and gave me a gift of a beautiful memorial book you could put mementos of your loved one in, and people who came could sign. Kristina stood at the door to allow people to sign the book as they entered the church.

As it was a memorial service there was no coffin and, as David suggested, we had a table at the front with carefully chosen favourite photos of Philip which the children helped me pick out. The church was packed with people saying goodbye to him. My parents and brother were there, as well as people representing the high school and primary school. With eight children, it's difficult for the whole school community not to be affected. There were flowers and tributes, and my lovely daughter, Sarah, at only 11 years of age, played Amazing Grace on her penny whistle. She never faltered.

But this wasn't a totally sad service, because we were also celebrating a life that was once lost and became found! Once a life that was committed to making money, and addicted to alcohol, to being totally surrendered to Christ, and to growing a family to God's glory! He left a legacy of eight incredible children, and countless grandchildren, and great grandchildren, to come whom, I believe, will be followers of Christ. This is not a story of hopelessness, but a story of victory!

I remember that verse in Psalm 116:15 where it says, *"Precious in the sight of the Lord are the death of His saints."*

Yes, God was rejoicing over his servant Phil, and so were the angels in Heaven! *"O death, where is your sting? O Hades, where is your victory?"* (1 Corinthians 15:55)

It was a sad, but beautiful day at the graveside, and it is the loveliest of cemeteries. The Sun shone through the trees and birds sang. I have seen many church yards, and have visited Westminster Abbey, as well as many other Cathedrals in the UK with those stark headstones and stone effigies, and I thank God for our small Beerwah cemetery where my husband's body lies. It is surrounded by pine plantations, and is quiet and peaceful. He was Canadian and he would be happy surrounded by pine forests.

They allowed us to drape the Australian flag over his coffin before putting it in the ground. He loved his adopted country, and its flag was, to him, a symbol of our Christian heritage. The Union Jack in the corner signifying our British Christian roots, with the crosses of St Patrick, St Andrew and St George. The three crosses are also a crossed cross, as we remember that Christ is the 'Alpha and Omega', the beginning and the end, the first and the last, the bright and Morning Star! The Southern Cross is also a Christian symbol – when the explorers saw it they marvelled that His sign was here too!

Remember the ladies I mentioned the day my husband died? The lady, whose husband would discuss the Bible with my husband, is one grave over. My friend, Flo's husband, is buried in another part of the cemetery, as is Flo herself now. Flo was a quiet servant of God who would prepare the flowers for the church service every Sunday, and would often give them to me to take home after. It was dear Flo who supplied all the flowers for the memorial service, and the church ladies who prepared the food. Our pastor took the service, and was very supportive. I have been blessed by God in so many ways!

There are other friends in that small cemetery too. My dear Christian friend, Ken, who also came to Christ late in life, but was the happiest most joyful person, and would lift your spirits when he greeted you at church. He struggled with smoking, and he finally got an invasive type of lung cancer. One day as his friend, Noelene, dropped him off at his caravan after a course of chemo, he sat in his favourite chair in the annexe, and was still there two days later after going to his Lord. He was the same age as Philip when he died.

My friend, Flo, who the children and I lived beside for a few years, refused to go to a nursing home, and died in her chair at home with her precious dog, Honey, beside her. God is good, and His mercies are everlasting, as these dear people, including my husband, were taken to be with their Saviour without any prolonged suffering.

There are also some sad stories in that small cemetery. A young married friend, who lost her battle with cancer after fighting it for many years. A friend of my sons, who grew up with them, and whom I would take to kid's club. He could not cope any longer, and took his own life. His mother, a dear Christian friend, used the funeral to speak to the young people, and admonish them to seek help if they were depressed or not coping. Like my daughter, Sarah, this young man grew up without a father. Yes, it is a special place that small cemetery, full of joy and deep sorrow.

I am reminded that this life is but a passing shadow and, in 2 Corinthians 4:18 it says, "*While we do not look at the things which are seen, but at the things which are not seen. For the things which are seen are temporary, but the things which are not seen are eternal.*"

Chapter 8

LIFE GOES ON

The family somehow got on with the task of living, and we struggled through as best we could. After the funeral we went to stay with my parents on the Gold Coast for a few days. I remember we took the children to the big 'Toys 'R Us' store at the Pacific Fair Shopping Centre. As I was walking around, I felt my chest begin to tighten, and I started to see the shop spin around me. The unrealistic thought struck me that I was going to die, just like my husband, and what then would happen to the children?

My father, sensing there was something wrong, came over and had me lean on him as he guided me out of the store. The centre management of the shops was close by, and I was able to sit down and was given a cup of tea. It was a panic attack, and a reaction to all the stress and shock I had suffered since Phil's death. We think we are coping well at these times, until our bodies tell us otherwise.

Sarah had made the regional cross-country team to compete at the state championships. It happened to be held on the Gold Coast that week. Thinking it may be a distraction for her, I allowed her to compete. The strange thing was that another girl had dropped out, leaving a spot for Sarah to compete at the cross country. To have it happen just after her dad died, and where my parents lived, seemed more than a coincidence. As we left the Gold Coast, it happened that her classmates had an outing planned for Dreamworld that day, and Sarah chose to go. The outing to the theme park happened as we were returning home. I can't help but wonder if this was all orchestrated by a loving God, to help us all cope with the immediate trauma of losing Phil.

A few months after Phil died, I had a photographer come to the door. He had an album of very special photos with him which had been taken of my husband, and the family. It was at a lovely park, called Kondalilla, where there are beautiful picnic grounds, and a walk down a valley to a very popular swimming hole called Kondallila Falls.

The story of these photos is very special. As I look back, I believe they were a small gift from God. Around Christmas there was a competition on at the local shopping centre. You filled out a form with your details, and it went in the draw for some prizes. Amongst these prizes was a photo shoot with a professional photographer. There were also vouchers to shop at many of the stores.

We were very excited and surprised to receive a phone call to say we had won! We collected our prizes, and then had to call the photographer to arrange a time for the photos. The photographer apologised that he had only just taken over the business, and it was the previous owner who had promised the shopping centre the photo shoot for the winners of the competition. It would take a couple of months before we would have our photos taken. By the time the photographer had met us at Kondallila Falls, my husband had known for a few months about the brain tumour. In between taking photos Phil would share his story with the photographer.

It was a beautiful day, and we had managed to have all eight of our children there. We went to different places in the park, and photographs were taken of the whole family, me and the girls, and Phil and the boys. The photographer also took a few of my husband and I.

We had said goodbye to the photographer, and drove back along the Blackhall range in our green van. There are beautiful views from the range, out to Caloundra and Maroochydore, and the ocean. It truly is an amazing spot, the Sunshine Coast of Queensland. There are beautiful sandy beaches with great surf, and also lovely spots, like Mooloolaba, for swimming. The Hinterland, where we lived, was home to Steve Irwin's Australia Zoo, and also the home of the beautiful Glasshouse Mountains, which used to be active volcanos. The mountains are also connected to aboriginal stories of the Dreamtime. Captain James Cook saw them from his ship, the Endeavour, naming them after the glass houses in England. There is also the Blackall range, with its amazing views and green fields. There are many art and craft shops, and places to eat and have coffee.

It was a lovely, pleasant drive until, as we were driving back to our home, the temperature gauge on the van shot up and we were forced to pull over! The radiator was empty, and it wasn't safe to drive down the hill to Beerwah. We had stopped in front of a lovely house on the main road. I have no doubt God was looking after us even then! A very nice lady came to the door, and my husband explained about the van and asked if we would be able to use their phone to ring the automobile club which, in Queensland, is the RACQ. The RACQ would play a role later, when Sarah was up in Bundaberg.

When she saw we had eight children, and it was a warm day, she invited us all in and gave us drinks. She introduced us to her husband, and we sat chatting until the RACQ arrived. It was a Sunday afternoon, a very busy time for roadside assistance. It would be a long while waiting for the tow truck to get the van back to Beerwah. This dear lady and her husband, whom we discovered belonged to the Landsborough Seventh Day Adventist church, ended up feeding all of us, and basically emptied their kitchen to give us a meal. They had a disabled daughter, and I was shown the special play equipment they had for her. This couple were such a blessing, and we thanked God for them, living right where the van broke down.

I had forgotten all about the photos, as so much had happened since they were taken, until the photographer rang me up and apologised for the delay in getting them to us. I had to explain to him that Phil had passed away a few months earlier, and he told me how sorry he was. He came round with the photographs of the family. How special they were to us at this time. To see the family together for the last time, and all those beautiful pictures. There was an album and a few photos in cardboard frames, but the most special one was in a wooden frame, and it was a black and white shot of my husband and I together. When he left, I cried and cried, thanking God for his provision of these special memories. At the time we won the competition we had no idea that Phil was to leave us, but I believe God knew and He prepared these memories beforehand for us to remember him by.

The children went back to school, and I had to decide what I was to do with my life. I had been out of the work force for some time, and had previously been a nurse. I decided to try some seasonal farm work, and a Christian farmer from church took me on as a strawberry packer. We sat on big stools in a shed, and packed strawberries into containers, putting them on conveyor belts to be weighed and put in boxes for the various places they would be sold. It was a great job for me, because I could start a little bit later to get the children off to school, and I could leave in time to be home and take them to athletics' training. It was also extremely tiring, as I wasn't used to sitting all day! I would get in the car and be crying with exhaustion some days. I did appreciate the money it brought in, and also the company of the other ladies.

During the school holidays I was allowed to bring in my twin sons, who were seven. My sons, Joe and Ben, although twins, look totally different and are opposites in many ways, but both extremely special young men. When their father was alive, they loved to help him out in the yard, raking the leaves or helping him with the latest project. The farm was a family business, and the owner's father would sit at the back of the shed supervising everyone. He loved the boys, and would allow them to help by emptying the less than perfect strawberries into big boxes. After work we could take some home, or the church ladies would make jam to sell to raise money for missions.

One day, Joe decided he wanted to put the strawberry containers into the boxes, and help pile them up ready for transport to Sydney or Melbourne. It was a few weeks later, when the truck driver was delivering the boxes, that they uncovered a completely empty box amongst the others. I don't think they were happy about the boys helping after that, but old Guy would just chuckle and give the boys the money he promised them. I was very fond of him, and eventually he too died of cancer. He is in the little cemetery with Phil.

After two years of struggling with strawberry work, I felt my children were old enough for me to make the decision to return to nursing. I could have studied through correspondence, or I could go to the university in Brisbane. I prayed about it, and felt God's assurance that I was more than capable. I chose to do a Graduate Certificate in Australian Nursing Studies at university, which would take six months. This was new to me, as I had done my nurses' training in the hospital system. I was then 46, and had little experience with computers and researching. Twice a week it would take over two hours of train and bus travel to reach the university, and then every second week I would have to get the early train at 0530 in the morning!

It was fortunate that the bus, which took the children to school, stopped right outside our house. I would spend every evening helping the children with their homework, and then make up six lunch boxes for school in the morning so they could just grab their lunch before getting the school bus. It was a challenge for me to do assignments, and cope with computer malfunctions, but somehow the Lord helped me get through. I would continue taking the children to athletics' training and competitions at weekends.

I met many women who, for one reason or another, were returning to nursing. One lady I met had been married to a high-flying business executive, and he became ill. This lady had given up her nursing career to travel the world with him. While she was nursing him one day, he told her that he believed nursing was what she was called to do and, after he died, she took the plunge like the rest of us and re-entered the nursing profession. It was to be another five months after I was registered, before I finally went back to work in a hospital. The ward was 3A, and was to be my home from home for the next 11 years. We called it the recycled ward because three of my friends, from my town of Beerwah, all went back to nursing as middle-aged women at the same time!

Chapter 9

THE CHILDREN

In the years since Phil died, the children and I coped the best we could. It is hard with a big family, and limited time to spend on each, but I did my best to give them my time and my love. Bringing up eight children has not been without its difficulties, but I would never dream of living without one of my precious children. Each are individuals, with special personalities and gifts given by God. I have been truly blessed, and I wonder at a God who can form so many different human beings in the same womb. Even my twins, who are fraternal, look so different that some people wondered if they were even brothers. One son had a friend who looked more like him than his twin brother!

My son, Ben, asked me one night, "Mum, will I ever see Dad again?"

I answered, "Ben, your dad is with Jesus in Heaven now, and when you give your heart to Jesus, you will see him again."

He said, "Mum, I do want to see him again, and I want to give my heart to Jesus."

I led my son to Jesus that night, at the age of seven, and I believe there will be ups and downs in my son's life, but that Jesus will never leave him or forsake him! From that time on I believe Father God became his dad, and has been with him since. He has also had a lot of positive input by Christian men in his life, from his pastor and males in our church, to the school chaplain who took the boys on a 'dudes without dads' camp. Ben has always been his own person, and is reserved, but not afraid to take on life's challenges.

One of Ben's great loves was athletics. He was athletics all-rounder at his high school, and became a decathlete representing Queensland. After university, Ben decided to go to Europe and live in Germany. He tackled the German language, and has become comfortable conversing with German speakers. He is not afraid to step out of his comfort zone, living and studying in Sweden while learning the language, and is now back in Australia. He was even learning to Salsa!

My son, Joe, is much like his father, and has a gift of being able to chat to people naturally. Everyone loves Joe as he has a giving heart, and an ability to make those he talks to feel special. He missed his father, but found friendship in an older man who was pastor of the Assembly of God church in our town. He always had a good word to say about Joe, and impacted him greatly.

The church used to run a breakfast programme at the primary school, so everyone knew Pastor Peel. He too has gone to be with the Lord. Joe now has two little girls of his own, and is determined to be a good dad because of losing his own father. Joe has battled a number of issues, but has never allowed himself to be defeated and, despite problems with his feet, has played Rugby League, Aussie Rules, and Touch football. He was a great dummy half, and even became a Touch referee!

Now I am not underestimating the problems that have arisen from the death of my son's father as there are still struggles for both these young men of mine, but through prayer and trusting God to lead them I know there will be victory for all my children!

Leah is my youngest daughter, and not only lost her father at the age of 10, but went through a difficult time when her sister was going through her problems. It is difficult for other children when most of the attention goes to the one who is struggling with life. Despite this, Leah has a natural love of God and, as soon as she was finished high school, put herself through Bible leadership college for two years, and then did two years of study to be a youth worker. She has been a chaplain in a Christian school, studied teaching, and then took a break to do YWAM, which is a youth missionary group on Kona, Hawaii. She completed the discipleship training school, and did her missionary trip to Peru.

She boated down the Amazon River, where they stopped at villages along the way, preaching the gospel and ministering to the Amazon tribes. What an adventure! They even went to a village where YWAM said they shouldn't go, but the Holy Spirit had other ideas and, at the time they were there, the village was mourning the death of an elder. This gave them opportunity to minister to the grieving. They approached one house where there was a sick baby, and so the group laid hands on the baby, and the spirit of God touched the child and the baby was healed! This opened the door for them to tell the tribe about Jesus.

God is so good, and He has also taken Leah to Thailand to help with a house they were renovating for girls rescued from sex slavery.

A man from her church was chosen, out of many applicants, to train with the renowned evangelist, Reinhardt Bonke. David was a business man with a heart for evangelism. Leah was given the chance to go on a crusade to Ethiopia with a group from her church that David led. What an amazing time she had, as the women ministered to women there, and then joined the men at the outreach where thousands of Ethiopians gave their hearts to

Christ, and were healed miraculously by the power of God! The worship shook the area, as thousands jumped up and down worshipping Jesus!

Leah got to pray for the sick and see so many healed. What a life this young woman has had, and it's not finished as now she is married to a young man of God and is celebrating the birth of their first son, named Isaiah, which means 'God saves'. They have since had a daughter named Abigail, which means 'the Father's heart'. This beautiful little girl couldn't wait to come into the world, and was delivered by her father on the front step of their unit! The timing couldn't have been more perfect, as I had taken big brother for a walk to the shops only about an hour before! When Leah, herself, was born there was a country show on that weekend near the hospital, and there were fireworks! I joke that God was so excited at Leah's birth He sent fireworks to celebrate her!

Jacob is my fourth child, and was just 13 when his father died. He was a talented saxophone player at school. Quiet as a boy, he never really talked much about his father. He met his wife, Alex, two years after losing his dad. When he got through high school, he did Engineering with honours at university. Alex was doing performing arts at the same university in Toowoomba, and they both joined a church there. Once they finished their degrees, they married at Maleny on the beautiful Sunshine Coast. They lived in London for three years, and Alex was the event manager for St. Paul's Anglican church in Hammersmith. They are now living a dream life in New York City! Jacob with his engineering experience in London, now works as an engineer in New York. Alex and Jacob have beautiful twin girls, and Alex is a very successful business woman. They both attend a church in Brooklyn, near where they live.

Aaron, at the time his dad died, was the eldest at home at 16, and has always been a quiet and thoughtful son. I think it was tough for him, as with most teenagers. There can be strife growing up as you desire to become more independent. He had quite long hair for a while, and was a middle-distance runner. Very well loved by his school friends. His father was always teasing him about his long hair, and getting it cut.

I used to say, "Phil, he will decide he's had enough and cut it off one day but, if you keep pressuring him, he will keep it!"

The day came when he decided he had had enough, and got it cut. I often think, when dealing with teenagers, about the verse in Ephesians 6:4, *"And you, fathers, do not provoke your children to wrath, but bring them up in the training and admonition of the Lord."* I think, as parents, we can make a lot of small issues, instead of leaving the big fights for the things that matter most. As a young boy, Aaron would remind me to pray for him before he went to school, and I would pray protection over him and for guidance during the day, as I did with all my children. My son has a degree in Sports Science, and later did a degree in engineering, achieving first class honours. He lives with his wife, Erin, in Brisbane now, where they both work in construction.

Esther is the second oldest in the family. She has a very gentle nature and, at the time her father died, she lived in Brisbane while studying for a science degree at the Queensland University of Technology. The campus is situated near the beautiful Brisbane River, and near the Brisbane Botanic gardens. She met her husband, Richard, there at a university Christian club. He was not from a Christian home, but discovered Christ while he was at high school in Tully. They have been married for over 20 years, are committed Christians, and have three amazing sons.

Naomi, my eldest child, was always rather strong-willed as a girl. I remember, when she went off to university, praying for her that she would follow the Lord. She ended up in a church which was very works-oriented, and never really talked about Grace. She used to come home all fired up, and wanting to preach at me. I remember wondering what on earth I had prayed for? However, I was just so glad she knew the Lord, and God changed her heart. She is a beautiful Christian and has been married for over 20 years, with three beautiful children. Naomi, and her husband Ben, run the youth group at their church, while she also leads worship, and a woman's Bible study.

We come to my fifth child, Sarah. This book is basically about her, and the struggles she had as a young girl, then as a teenager, and finally as a young adult. She was 11 years old the year her father died, and the school captain at her primary school. A very high achiever, like her brothers and sisters, but more of a perfectionist then any of the others. Despite losing her father that year, she would play in the school band, become the highest academic achiever, and also become female sports' champion. With hair down to her waist, and an amazing confidence at just 12 to speak in public, she would give her end-of-year speech, even making mention of her father.

You hope that, as a parent, you can convey to your children how to live responsible lives, and to get through the pitfalls of growing up. I am again reminded of scripture that says to, *"train up a child in the way he should go and, when he is old, he will not depart from it."* (Proverbs 22:6)

I laugh when I read this, as it leaves out the in between bit of when they are 'teenagers'! God knew that the changes which would take place in a growing young person would not always be easy but, to give them a good Christian upbringing while they are young, is essential for the life they would live as adults. I can't imagine Mary putting up with Jesus sulking! Take heart parents, and keep praying!

I want to say how proud I am of all my children, and their various achievements. God has blessed them with amazing gifts and talents!

Chapter 10

GOD WATCHES OVER US AND MIRACLES DO HAPPEN

For a period of two years, when my two eldest were small, it felt like we were in some sort of war for survival. While growing up as a young girl, Naomi escaped death and severe injury many times. It was almost like a concerted attack on her, and I would pray protection over her, and her sister, every day.

She was hit by a car once when walking across a quiet back street with her father. One minute she would be holding her father's hand, and the next she was lying across the road face down. A car had come out of a driveway, and the small car hit the side of her. The miracle was that, apart from her bottom teeth going through her upper lip, there was no other injury!

Another time she ran away from me at our unit in Melbourne, and ran straight onto a busy road. I thought I would lose her for sure, and asked God to save her. The cars slowed down just in time. A third time I was at my parent's place in Perth, and my mother had gone down to meet my father as he got off the bus with the two girls. Esther was a baby in the stroller, and Naomi was walking beside holding the stroller handle. They left the house and, as I was doing the dishes, I had a picture in my mind of Naomi running out in front of a car.

I quickly put the thought out of my head so as not to worry and said aloud, "I rebuke you Satan. She is under the blood of the lamb!"

Shortly after, my mother came into the house with my father and the girls, visibly shaken. She could hardly speak, she was so angry and upset! Mum told me that they had gone round the corner after leaving the house, and were preparing to cross a very quiet street that had a slight hill. My mum started pushing the stroller across, when Naomi screamed and grabbed at her clothes, holding her back. Just at that moment a car came tearing over the hill, and would most certainly have hit all three of them. Was it an angel that caused Naomi to react?

James 4:7 says: *"Therefore submit to God. Resist the devil and he will flee from you."*

I rebuked the Devil, and let him know that I placed her under the blood of Jesus! These weren't the only mishaps between the ages of three and five. She fell in my parent's pool and could have drowned, ran into the middle of the Hills hoist, split open her head, and slipped running up the steps splitting her chin open!

Before this we had lived in Papua New Guinea, and even there we had a few almost fatal mishaps. Naomi got malaria, and was very sick. I would crush up the quinine tablets, and put them in a chocolate drink, called 'Milo' in Australia. My daughter couldn't have got enough quinine. Later, in Australia, there would be a few times she would get unexplained fevers, but they soon stopped.

Her sister, Esther, was playing in the neighbour's garden one day when we lived in PNG. There is a narrow ditch between the yards, with a plank of wood that goes across for you to walk on. At just 18 months of age, Esther had found a pair of hedge clippers and picked them up. The blades were open, and the hinge caught on her dress. She walked home with the hedge clippers open across her neck and chest. When I found her, Esther had toddled across the plank into our garden. If she had fallen over she may not have been alive today!

I was also miraculously spared from death. I had been folding clothes by a backyard window, and had sat down for a minute. One of the local chaps was mowing our back lawn. As I sat down, something came flying through the window with a crash. It turned out to be a loose blade off the lawn mower, which would have hit me in the back of the head. Again, I thank God for saving me. My mother woke up in the middle of the night praying for me around this time. I believe the angels were looking after us, as it says in Psalm 91:11, *"For He shall give His angels charge over you, to keep you in all your ways."*

As a girl at the age of seven, I had been out playing in the neighbourhood where I lived in Vancouver, Canada. I was standing at the entrance to a back lane, when a car crossed the road and stopped in front of me. It was a white station wagon, and I can still remember what this man looked like. He lowered the window and asked if I wanted a lift in his car. I remember freezing, and didn't answer him when he asked me again to get in his car. At that point I knew he was a stranger, and potentially dangerous, so I turned and ran home as quick as I could. I was glad my parents had warned me about stranger danger but, also looking back, very grateful to God that His angels were watching over me. I may not have been here to write this book, or have my eight children!

My daughter, Esther, and her husband Richard, struggled to have children, and went through fertility treatment for many years. My daughter had bad endometriosis and, even after surgery, it was still difficult for her to conceive. Finally, after much investigation and prayer, they found a Christian IVF doctor, and decided on IVF treatment. They chose to have fewer eggs fertilised than usual so that they could use all of the embryos, and not discard any. Some of the medical staff were not very supportive of this, but Esther and Richard felt that God could use fewer embryos and, if they did not fall pregnant, it would be God's will.

With five frozen embryos on hand, they had the first one implanted and soon after discovered they were pregnant. My grandson's name is Theodore, and he is very special. It means 'A Gift from God'. The second embryo was implanted about a year after Theo was born. That day I sat in the park watching Theo, while Esther and Richard had the procedure done, and I prayed to God for their success. A few weeks later, again a baby was conceived, and he would be called Philip, after Esther's dad. The doctor told Esther and Richard that they had spoiled his statistics! Although the next three embryos were implanted, they would not produce a baby, but all five embryos had been used, and none discarded.

It was decided that Esther would have surgery again, and have a last try to conceive naturally. I decided to do something to express my faith in God for the conception of their baby number three. I started to knit a baby blanket for the baby to come and, as I knitted, I would pray for God's miraculous intervention. I finished the blanket and stored it away, before going to the UK. Four months after I left Australia, and before Esther had any surgery, she rang me to let me know that they were pregnant. Baby boy number three on the way. How good is God! I love the scripture that, in Hebrews 11:1, says: *"now faith is the substance of things hoped for, the evidence of things not seen."* It continues in Hebrews 11:6, *"But, without faith, it is impossible to please Him, for he who comes to God must believe that He is, and that He is a rewarder of those who diligently seek Him."* Beautiful baby Zachary was born, and mum and dad were so grateful to God for this new miracle.

Chapter 11

MY TWO ELDEST GIRLS GET MARRIED

Less than two years after my husband's death, my daughters, Naomi and Esther, had some special news for me. In consultation with their respective fiancés, they had both decided to get married – and in the same year! Esther and Richard in January 2002, and Naomi and Ben in June 2002. I had been a widow for just 18 months, and had very little money in the way of savings. But both my daughters were determined that they were going to get married that year. I definitely had to trust God with this dilemma.

My favourite verse at times like this is Phil. 4:19, *"And my God shall supply all your need according to his riches in glory by Christ Jesus."*

And He did just that!

The first area of need was a wedding dress for Esther. I had been invited to attend a Christian conference at a centre at Mt Tambourine, a beautiful spot in the mountains near Queensland's Gold Coast. It was a year after Phil died, and it was good for me to go to a Christian gathering and meet new people. A few of us were out walking around the shops in town, and having coffee together, when one of the ladies started to talk about her daughter's wedding. It was mentioned that she had made her daughter's dress, and it had fitted her perfectly but, as the wedding day approached, her daughter had started taking the contraceptive pill. One of the side-effects was weight gain. Trying on the dress again before the wedding it was discovered that it no longer fitted! This lady had this beautiful wedding dress which had never been worn.

I casually asked if I could perhaps have a look at it, because my daughter was getting married the following January and did not have a dress yet. It turned out that this lady only lived 10 minutes from my house, and yet we met at a place some two-hours away! I rang up and arranged to see the dress. It was beautiful, and looked like Esther's size. The next thing was to have my daughter see it, and that was arranged. When Esther saw the dress she exclaimed it was just the kind of dress she had always dreamed of. When she tried it on, it fitted her like a glove! The lovely lady who made it only asked three hundred dollars for it and, as part of my contribution, I said I would pay for it. I was even allowed to pay it off in instalments. Praise God for his first provision!

The next thing would be bridesmaids' dresses for my girls. It so happened that a lady across the road was a seamstress, and offered to make the dresses for Sarah and Leah. She did an amazing job, and for half the cost of getting them made elsewhere. This kind lady would also make the bridesmaid dresses for Naomi's wedding too.

Richard's family paid for the wedding reception, and our meal with family afterwards, of which I am very grateful. It was planned that the main reception would be a simple afternoon tea. The wedding itself would take place at the large Baptist Tabernacle in Brisbane city. Downstairs in the church's basement was where the caterers would serve the afternoon tea. Two weeks before the wedding there was panic, as Esther and Richard realised that there would not be room for 200 people in the basement, which would be unbearably hot as it was the middle of summer! The Brisbane Town Hall was a few blocks away from the church, and they had rooms to let for receptions. What an answer to prayer, as the Ball Room was available, and it would be air conditioned, something that was not available in the church basement. Not only was there space, the venue could also cater for the afternoon tea, and had a bar at the back! God was so good to allow us to hire this beautiful hall at the last minute, but there was still more provision to come.

January in Australia, especially in Queensland, tends to be extremely hot and humid. It was true to form, and it turned out to be a 40-degree day with high humidity. Esther's university church was helping with the wedding, and members even sang at the ceremony. Esther's house, that she shared with university friends, had no air conditioning, and a lovely couple from her church suggested the bride, bridesmaids, and mother of the bride (myself) would go to their beautiful home which was air conditioned. It had been a fundraising home which had been purchased from the people who had won it, so as you can imagine, it was beautiful. Not only did we all have our makeup and hair done there, but this kind lady supplied us all with lunch. She even ironed dresses!

The photographer was another blessing as he was a friend of Esther's. Richard and Esther only had to pay for the photos and negatives. Some of the most beautiful photos were taken in the house where Esther and the bridesmaids got ready.

The day arrived, and Esther was walked down the aisle by her grandfather. Leah, at only 11, would lead the procession. It was the first wedding in the family, and it was everything a bride could dream of. Esther made such a gorgeous bride, and Richard looked so handsome in his suit waiting at the front. It was a very hot day, but God was there at the beautiful ceremony of this lovely Christian couple.

Photos were taken in the Brisbane Botanical Gardens and, despite the heat, they turned out beautifully. Finally we headed for the town hall, and the reception, which was wonderfully cool after the heat outside. The food was excellent, and the guests really enjoyed themselves. A special moment came when my son-in-law walked towards a baby grand piano in the spacious reception room and sat down, to play the piano and sing a song to my daughter. It was a Beatles song called, 'Till there was you'. What a special moment, as everyone stood speechless listening to this young man pour out his heart into this tribute to his new wife. Esther was unaware that Richard played the piano, and he had kept secret the weeks of rehearsing for that magic moment.

My eldest daughter, Naomi, and her fiancé, Ben, married in June during Australia's winter. It is usually cold at night and early morning, but during the day it can be very warm and pleasant. Naomi was very artistic and, at one time, she wanted to be involved in fashion design. She decided to design her own wedding dress, and it was beautifully made of silk. It was like a medieval dress, and it came in at her slim waist. It was stunning! Naomi has the pale skin, dark curly hair, and blue eyes of the Celts. The beautiful dress suited her so well, and the bridesmaid's dresses were in dark green. It was to be a garden wedding, and people from Naomi and Ben's church had even landscaped their lovely country garden for the event. The wedding party had their hair and makeup done in the house, with the fire going as the morning was cool. When all the guests were assembled, Naomi would come out of the house with the bridesmaids, and walk down the stairs into the garden towards her husband under the trees. It was my honour to accompany my daughter, and be the one to give her away.

The weather was kind, being a perfect winter day with the sun shining. Naomi's church choir sang without music (a cappella), and they were amazing. At the ceremony, my twin boys had the rings. Somehow they got mixed up, and were given to the wrong person, which caused a few giggles. It was a beautiful ceremony, and they both read the vows that each had written for the other. When the time came to kiss the bride it was an extra special moment, as they had never kissed each other all the time they had been dating. They would hold hands and look into each other's eyes, but never kissed.

Abstinence before marriage is something rarely seen in today's society. Esther and Richard waited until they got married before they were intimate. I think it is special, and I know that before we come to Christ, we don't often understand the consequences of sleeping together outside of marriage. God is faithful, and will forgive us our sins, and can restore what is taken, but it takes desire and discipline in putting God first. Please don't ever think my family are perfect, because we aren't. We all need to know the Saviour, and be forgiven, for there is no-one without sin. The fact is, we miss out on the joy of what waiting can bring. More and more young people are taking vows of chastity before marriage, which is a lovely thing.

The church members had banded together and supplied the three-course meal, which was set up in the back garden. God is so good. Naomi and Ben took off on their honeymoon with the cans at the back of the car bouncing all over the road! Two perfect weddings, and a God who supplied all of our needs!

Ephesians 3:20 says, *"Now to Him who is able to do exceedingly abundantly above all that we ask or think, according to the power that works in us, to Him be glory in the church by Christ Jesus to all generations, forever and ever. Amen."*

Chapter 12

TURMOIL IN THE CAMP

A number of things happened in the following years that, I believe, were upsetting for the four younger children. We had lived in the same house for 11 years. It was where my twins were born, and it was where we lived when Phil passed away. It was a great house for growing children, with a big back yard, and the school bus would stop at the front door. The owners were siblings, and sent me a letter regretting that they would have to sell the house. They were sorry that we would have to move, as we had been such good tenants. The rent was manageable where we lived, and to find something else would mean more money. I wasn't nursing yet, and could not afford much more in rent.

Another painful thing I had to do was clear a house out of things collected during the 11 years we had been living there! My husband was always stockpiling papers, books and documents, for when he would get round to writing that article or book. There were so many books on Christianity, and more boxes of things in the garage. I felt anxious just thinking of trying to get rid of it all!

I firstly advertised the books locally, and a man came round who was studying the Bible. I was grateful to him because he ended up buying two car-loads of books. Yes, two car loads of books, and that was after me keeping many that I was still interested in.

I also contacted a book shop in a town nearby, and they purchased a few boxes of books too. Next was the garage. If I had gone through all the tea chests and boxes, I would have found it hard to part with things. Thankfully, my eldest son, Aaron, took charge, and just threw most of it out. I don't know to this day what was in half of them, and I realised I couldn't miss something I didn't know existed!

I am also thankful for the people in the small Methodist church that we were part of. When it came to the task of moving me and the children, and all our belongings, you could not have found a better bunch of helpers. My friends, Fiona and her husband Neil, who lived across the creek from us, even helped with the cleaning. As did my good friends, Judy and David. Poor David got the shock of his life when in the family room. I had brought the lawn mower and the grass catcher in the house, so they wouldn't get stolen while we were moving. In fact, a ladder leaning against the back wall did get stolen. While David was busy doing some final cleaning jobs, he happened to look in the grass catcher, and was shocked when he saw a huge carpet python curled up in it. They are harmless, as there is no poison in them, but they are big, and could squeeze a small animal to death!

There are plenty of snakes in Australia, and we lived near one of the world's most famous zoos that has many different species on display. Australia Zoo is the home of the late Steve Irwin, known to most people overseas as 'The Crocodile Hunter'. My friend, David, who found the carpet snake, went to school with him as a boy. Steve apparently always had some interesting creatures in his pockets. He had a television program that was broadcast to millions every week. People everywhere loved the larrikin

TURMOIL IN THE CAMP

Aussie, who did crazy things like wrestling crocodiles. He was also a great wildlife conservationist, and bought up large tracks of land in Queensland to conserve native habitat. Tragically, he was killed in a freak accident while filming in the Great Barrier Reef marine park. He was scuba diving above a stingray and its barb went in his chest. He died almost instantly. It was a traumatic time for the Beerwah community, and all the workers at the zoo. My daughter worked there, and was able to get me a ticket to his memorial service that was broadcast worldwide.

In telling this story it is interesting to note that, at the time of Steve's death, I was involved in a spiritual warfare prayer group. I had come to know about the group when looking for answers to helping my daughter, Sarah. They often did prayer walks in areas, and I had been part of a small team of four who had been prayer-walking the nearby town of Landsborough.

We had finished, and were going to debrief back at the Baptist church, when we approached the entrance to the zoo. I felt God wanted us to pray for the zoo, so we pulled over into the car park. We sat and asked the Lord to show us what to pray for, and felt He wanted us to pray for the workers, staff, and their families. We sat and prayed for the zoo staff, and then drove back to Beerwah. Two weeks later, I woke up on a Monday morning to the news that Steve was dead, stung by the stingray barb! What a shock for our community. Steve was larger than life, and very missed by those who knew him. There would be feelings of grief worldwide for Steve, and condolences for his wife, Terry, daughter Bindi, and son Robert.

As well as the zoo, we had prayed at a particularly bad intersection where many lives had been lost, and also for the removal of a wooden idol that was on a road island. The road was a gateway to the Blackall range, and the towns of Maleny and Montville. There is a lot of witchcraft in those areas, so we felt that the presence of this idol was spiritually damaging.

Today there are now traffic lights at the intersection, and the Main Roads Department removed the ugly wooden idol which had also been next to a child's playground. Repentance was also offered to God for the Aboriginal blood that had been spilt in that place.

Chapter 13

A NEW HOME, BUT NOT FOR LONG

We finally found a new home, at a higher rent, but it was better than most places. It was a lovely house, and we had our own dam which you could swim in, and even row a small boat. It meant moving from Beerwah to the nearby town of Glasshouse Mountains. The children had a bit further to travel to school but, again the bus stopped right at the front of the house. My daughter's friend, Sarah, lived nearby. They were both good at athletics, and competed together. Her friend's father was a member of the Federal government, and he has been such a blessing to the family. Mal was very down to earth, and genuinely cared for his constituents.

I had mentioned to his wife that I was anxious about finding a place to rent. The Prime minister at the time was John Howard. At one point they even considered buying a house we could have rented from them. Another time I approached Mal at a school fête to ask if he knew of a way I could get funding for my son, Jacob, to travel with the school band to New Zealand. He said if Jacob made an effort to raise some of the money he would see what he could do. I expected that, with all of Mal's commitments, he would forget all about the encounter. Imagine my surprise when he rang to say he had the money for Jacob.

Shortly after Phil died I had gone to the Brisbane agricultural show, known as the EKKA (short for 'exhibition'). I couldn't afford to take the children, so I went by myself and promised to buy them some showbags. As I was looking at the gardening exhibit, I noticed that the radio station was there interviewing a couple of politicians. One happened to be Mal, so I sat down to listen, and realised I was the only one there at the time. As I was listening, he looked up and saw me sitting in the audience and then, unbelievably, mentioned me on the radio, and that I had a very clever daughter, called Sarah. I couldn't believe he would interrupt the program to talk about my family and I. After he was finished, he introduced me to the other politician he had been interviewed with.

Life has not been easy, but God has blessed us along the way with friends like Mal, my church family, and many others who prayed with me.

The owners of the new house were an English couple who seemed very friendly. They couldn't do enough for us. We had a six-month lease and, at the time we took the house with the dam, there was another house we looked at across the road. It had very tall trees in the front yard, and seemed very dark inside. It was rented by a young couple with small children who would not have appreciated a dam in the back yard, as it would have been unsafe. I later found out that Mary, a friend of mine, owned the house, but we had already signed a lease.

The younger girls, Sarah and Leah, loved the house because they had a converted granny flat to themselves, with an air conditioner and a toilet. We could sit out on the covered deck, look at the water, and watch all the bird life come and go. It was very relaxing. Just after we moved in, I started work at a hospital about 20 minutes' drive away at the nearby town of

Caboolture. The boys didn't mind living in Glasshouse, and everything seemed to be working out as I was now earning a bit more money.

While we were living at Glasshouse Mountains, I received a call from a representative of the Coca Cola company saying that I had been nominated as a finalist in a competition to carry the Olympic Torch at the 2004 Athens torch relay, in Melbourne. I was astounded! What had I done to be nominated? I found out that Phoebe, the daughter of my friends Judy and David, had suggested to her mother that I would be a good candidate to nominate, and they had entered me in the competition. I was a finalist, and they asked me lots of questions about my life, and needed permission to use me in the advertising for the torch relay. It was the one good thing that kept me going when the bomb fell.

We had only been at the new house about three months when I received a letter in the mail from the real estate agent. It was to tell me that the rent would go up after the first six months to an extra $25 a week. It was a shock because, although I was managing the rent now, to pay another $25 was a huge increase. Unfortunately, the wife of the landlord chose that day to ring me about some new curtains she wanted to put up in one of the bedrooms.

The timing could not have been worse, and I told her about the letter from the real estate agent, and said I didn't know if I was going to be able to afford it. I did not expect the reaction I got, and almost the next day received a letter from the real estate agent to say that our lease would be terminated at the end of the six-month period. We would have to find somewhere else to live! I was given no chance to accept the new lease conditions because of what I had said to the owner's wife. I was now beginning to realise what a nightmare of a landlord I had! I did not know what to do, as we had only just moved in, and it had been such a huge move for us. I tried to reason with the real estate agent, but they were just following the landlord's orders. Although we paid the rent on time, and looked after the property, I believe we were made to look like the worst of the worst tenants!

I later realised that the real estate agent had difficulty renting the property, so they would put down the rent to get someone in the property, and then put the rent up when the lease was due. The ironic thing was that, the young couple who had moved into my friend Mary's house across the road, had left owing almost three month's rent! I contacted Mary, and she said she was happy for our family to rent her house if the owner of the house we were in would allow us out of the lease agreement, and allow us to move right away.

I rang him, thinking he would be happy because he could get someone in the house as soon as we were gone, and they would pay the rent he wanted. He told me that he would not allow me out of the lease agreement, and I would have to stay there until the end of the lease which was another two months. The stress I was under was enormous, and I was made to feel like a criminal. Mary told me that, although she wanted to rent the house out to me, she needed a tenant in the house right away to recoup the rent that she had lost. As the time drew near for us to leave, there was nowhere that I could find that we could afford.

I rang the owner and said, "This is Roberta from your rental at Glasshouse, and I wondered if we could stay here, pay the increase in rent while we look for another house? I have six children, and it isn't easy finding another place!"

Instead of being met with some understanding of our situation, I was threatened over the phone with him saying, "I will get the police if you don't leave my premises at the end of the lease!"

As a Christian, this sort of attitude was such a shock to me. He even hired another real estate agent in the next town, and must have impressed on them how terrible we were. I later found out that we were under our rights to stay until we found somewhere, or until the rent court case came up. I was determined to leave, as this man was very vindictive, and I worried at what the stress was doing to my children and myself. The day before the lease expired, I discovered a letter which had been hand delivered and put in the mailbox. It was threatening me that, if I didn't leave by midnight that night, he would get the police to get me out! I kept that letter.

I can't begin to tell you how totally desolate I felt. I had been 11 years in the last house, with a wonderful reference, and now was being kicked out for an innocent remark I had made over the phone. My church was very supportive, and it was the church that was there, helping us move out the day the threatening letter was put in the mail box. I shed many tears at this time and, while reading my Bible one day, I came across a verse of Scripture in Psalm 56:8-9 which says: *"You number my wanderings; put my tears into your bottle; are they not in your book? When I cry out to You, then my enemies will turn back; This I know, for God is for me."*

I just had to keep going the best I could. We still had nowhere to go. Friends of mine had a two-story house, with a large granny flat, where my friend's mother lived. She was a beautiful elderly Christian lady, called Maud. I was to stay there with Maud with my two boys, while my two girls, Leah and Sarah, would stay with my friends, David and Judy, and with their two daughters. It was not an ideal situation, but I was determined that I was not going to be intimidated any more by that landlord, and would have lived in a tent if needed.

As my son Jacob was mowing the lawn one day after we moved out, the landlord told him he had to remove all the grass clippings from around the trees. It was then that my 17-year-old son bravely stood up to this man, and told him that he had caused his mother a lot of grief by how he had treated me. The landlord made the excuse that it was the fault of the real estate agent!

The morning we moved out, the landlord stood across the car park with his arms crossed, staring at me, with another real estate agent with him also looking intimidating as I handed in the keys. Later, this new real estate agent would apologise to me and my family for the way we had been treated, as she realised that this landlord, and his wife, were trouble makers and extremely difficult to work with. She would go out of her way to help us find a house in the area. No real estate agents in the immediate area would deal with them in the end, and they had to go further afield to get a real estate agent that would take them on.

The two older boys would move out, as one was at university, and the eldest, Aaron, had a job in Brisbane. It turned out that months later the threatening letter, that had been put in the mailbox that day, would come back to haunt that landlord.

Despite the hurt and stress I suffered at the hands of the couple who owned that house, I felt God wanted me to forgive them. I did this before we actually left the property, and wrote a letter to them which I left with the real estate agent explaining that I was sorry if I had upset anyone and, even though I was extremely upset at being evicted, I forgave them. To forgive them was the only way I could get closure for myself and move on. The Scripture says in Matthew 6:15, *"But if you do not forgive men their trespasses, neither will your Father forgive your trespasses."*

The poor Christian couple, who moved in after us, would soon find out what myself and my children had had to suffer. The garage, that had been converted into a granny flat, was very close to a gravel driveway where there was a small strip of grass in front. The gentleman was mowing the grass, when the lawn mower got too close to the gravel drive, causing a rock to fly up, breaking one of the glass sliding doors. When this happens, the landlord's insurance usually pays for repairs and, sometimes, the tenant may have to pay the excess. But, as we know, this landlord was not at all reasonable, and told the man if he didn't pay the whole cost of the broken glass door, he would take him to court!

The tenant had a very sick wife, and was extremely stressed by the menace of this landlord. He was taken to court, and the court said that it was up to the landlord's insurance to pay for the broken glass door. This was not good enough for this landlord and his wife, and they took the matter to a higher court! It was then that this Christian man and his wife, contacted me because they had heard about how poorly we had been treated. I told them that I would pray for them, and gave them a photocopy of the letter that had been put in my mailbox. They were able to take it with them to court to show the judge this man's character. God is our righteous judge, and he sees our trouble.

Psalm 6:8-10 says: *"Depart from me, all you workers of iniquity: for the Lord has heard the voice of my weeping. The Lord has heard my supplication; the Lord will receive my prayer. Let all my enemies be ashamed and greatly troubled: let them turn back and be ashamed suddenly."*

Chapter 14

A NEW HOME AND A TORCH RELAY

It was another blow for my younger children having to move into temporary accommodation until we could find a permanent home. I was separated from Leah 13, and Sarah 14, for a few months while we waited on the Lord for a place of our own again.

Having to share a small flat wasn't so bad. My friend, Maud, was such a sweet Christian lady. The warmth and joy of Christ was all too apparent in her. She also had a sharp wit, and keen sense of humour, and I enjoyed her company immensely. I continued working shift work at the hospital, making sure my boys got to school in Beerwah. I missed my girls, and couldn't see them very often, but knew they were in good hands at my friend, Judy's.

Then one day I received a phone call.

"Hello, is that Roberta Brown?"

"Yes, it is. Can I help you?"

"It's a representative from Coca Cola here, and we would like to inform you, Mrs Brown, that you have been chosen to carry the Olympic torch in Melbourne next year for the 2004 Olympic games!"

A NEW HOME AND A TORCH RELAY

"I'm so thrilled. Thank you so much!"

"We will send you all the information in the days ahead and, Mrs Brown, you have two tickets to Melbourne so you can bring someone with you. Congratulations."

I couldn't believe that I was to carry the torch and, in the middle of a painful experience, God had been preparing a blessing just for me! Although my situation seemed hopeless, God was at work, allowing me to fly to Melbourne to take part in an historic Olympics. It would be the first time the torch was carried across all continents. It would finally arrive in Athens on the 13th August – my birthday. My leg of the relay would be at the Docklands in Melbourne, in June. It was so exciting for me, as Coca Cola bought the torches on our behalf, and we were able to keep them as a memento of this time.

The reason I was chosen was for my volunteering with the local Little Athletics club, which six of my children were involved in. I was an official, recorder, and coach. I also had sports medicine training. They included my volunteering in my church and, I guess, the fact that I was a widow with a large family, helped them to decide on me. I was very blessed to have been chosen, because I am sure there would have been many more worthwhile candidates. The last year had been such a difficult one, so to enjoy a week in Melbourne, and be part of something so big, was amazing.

God was to send us another blessing, this time a home for myself and my children. Before I went to Melbourne, we found out that there was a house coming available across from the primary school in Beerwah. It was a private rental and, unbelievably, the rent would be $90.00 cheaper per week than if we had stayed in Glasshouse. It was an older house, and had a huge open lounge with rooms off of it. It would be cold in winter, and warm in summer, but was on a secluded bush block close to town. Rooms were made up by putting wardrobes and shelf units up as walls to give privacy. My friend Flos' house, was through a bush path next door. She would come to depend on us a bit, especially if her dog Honey was picked up by the pound, as she would keep running off.

I felt really blessed to be there, and very thankful to God that it was so cheap. As a family, this meant we could do more together. I could pay for their school excursions, and trips to Brisbane and Townsville where they would compete at the State Little Athletic titles. The lady who owned the house lived, and worked, as a teacher in Hong Kong. The upside was it had space, and was cheap rent, but the downside was there was little privacy for the two girls, and it wasn't as nice as the Glasshouse Mountains house. As a teenage girl this, I'm sure, was a disappointment for Sarah. It was to be in this house that my daughter would struggle, and the fight for her life would be fought.

It came time for my trip to Melbourne, and I was so excited! It was decided that my friend, Judy, would come with me. It would have been nice to have my children there, but I couldn't afford to bring them all, and didn't want to have to choose who went. We were put up in a room at the Crowne Plaza Hotel, opposite the Star Casino. Judy and I met many of the other torch bearers in the lobby of the Crowne, which added to the excitement. I met another lady from the Sunshine Coast who, with myself, would be in an article in the local Sunshine Coast paper. A bus would later take us to the Lord Mayor's reception that night at the Melbourne Town Hall.

It was a Gala affair and many famous sports stars and celebrities would be there. We were given our bags with our torch relay outfit. It was winter in Melbourne, so we had a white tracksuit and two jackets. One from the torch relay organisers, and my favourite one from the Coca Cola company with the worldwide route of the relay on the back. It seemed such a dream. The famous Australian Olympic basketball player, Andrew Gaze, was there and he would be the final torch bearer in Melbourne. He was to light the cauldron in Melbourne's Federation Square. He is also a well-known Christian, and a lovely man.

As Judy and I watched the entertainment, and had a drink with some nibbles, I saw a lady being wheeled around in a wheelchair. I was looking at this lady, and wondering where I knew her from. I suddenly realised she was the famous Betty Cuthbert, known to many as the 'Golden Girl' of Australian athletics. It was so strange to see her here as, the year before while walking through the mall in Brisbane, I saw a book store with a rack out the front with some discounted books in it. I put my hand in and grabbed a book. The title was 'Golden Girl', the story of the Olympian Betty Cuthbert! This was not a Christian book store and, imagine my surprise after buying the book, to read it and discover, not only was it a story of her life as a runner, but it was also her witness of her personal faith in Christ. And here she was in front of me, in the Melbourne Town Hall!

I had to meet this incredible lady who, despite battling Multiple Sclerosis for so many years, had an amazing smile that would light up the room. An incredible outpouring of her love of Christ.

"It's Betty Cuthbert, isn't it?" I asked

Her carer replied, "Yes, it is."

"Hello Betty, I have just read your incredible story, and it was an amazing testimony of your faith in the Lord. I too am a Christian, and wondered if I could get a picture of you and I?"

Betty smiled her incredible smile at me, and her carer said she would be happy to take a photo of us both.

I knelt beside her, and had a picture with her and her companion carer, Rhonda Gillam, who would sign Betty's autograph on her behalf. I was so overcome with the emotion of it all. I thought You are an amazing God and, despite all the setbacks of the last four years, He continued to amaze me with His goodness.

In Betty's book she talks about her trip to Scotland where I was born, and visiting two churches there, where the same hymn was sung. It was a favourite of mine called 'Take my Life' and it goes: "Take my life and let it be consecrated Lord to Thee."

A verse that jumped out at Betty as a runner was: "Take my feet and let them be swift and beautiful for Thee."

Betty won three gold medals at the Melbourne Olympic games in 1956 when I was only one year old, and a further Olympic gold in Tokyo in 1964. She held 16 world records. She would carry the torch at the 2000 Sydney Olympics, and then carry it again at the Melbourne Cricket Ground for the 2004 Olympic games in Athens. This is where our paths would cross and, along with many Australian greats of the sporting world, I, Roberta Brown, an unknown from the Sunshine Coast of Queensland, would be among them!

At breakfast the next day I would sit and eat beside the great Ron Barrassi, an icon of Australian Rules football who played and coached for many years. I would be carried on a bus through Melbourne, as we dropped off torch relay bearers along the route. Many were Olympic athletes from previous Olympic games and many, like myself, were involved in some way in their communities. The sad thing was that we were not allowed to carry anything with us but our torches, so I couldn't take pictures along the route. One of the highlights of the bus trip through Melbourne was passing an open tram carrying more of the Aussie greats of sport, among them Herb Elliot and Ron Clarke, both middle distance runners, as well as Dawn Fraser, the famous Australian swim star.

The Olympics was returning to Greece where it all first began, and Melbourne had a very large Greek community. The bus stopped in the centre of

A NEW HOME AND A TORCH RELAY

the Greek community's celebrations, where the Lord Mayor would address the crowd. They had Greek dancing, and plenty of Greek food. We would not be able to get off the bus, but had people yell and wave to us, as they recognised that we would be carriers of the Olympic flame.

Finally, it would be my turn to have my torch lit, and run the 400 metres with it to the next torch bearer. First of all, I had to disembark a few hundred metres from the exchange point, as the bus was unable to drop me there. So, with the security guard by my side, we ran down a side street to get to the corner where the Olympic yachtsman would meet me. I stood ready at the Docklands, where a few people gathered on their balconies to watch. As the world-renowned yachtsman tilted his torch towards mine, the man with me turned on my gas cylinder, and I leant in to light my torch from his flame.

What a moment for me! There weren't many spectators at that particular corner, except for a group on a balcony who yelled, "torch bearer, look up" and I looked up to see people cheering me on. Next, I had to run 400 metres to pass the flame on to a young Greek Australian girl who had won a writing competition. I wondered how I would keep pace, and jogged down the road with security guards and all the press on the back of a truck in front of me. I had to concentrate on holding the torch upright, as at one point the flame nearly went out.

As I passed the flame to the young Greek Australian girl, Judy was there to meet me with her video camera rolling. Soon after, the pickup bus would pick me up to take us back to the hotel. Judy told me later that, as she was waiting for me, her camera wouldn't work and she prayed that God would get it working before I arrived, which he did! What an amazing day. I cannot begin to explain how incredibly blessed I felt. Nagging at the back of my mind, though, was a question mark, and I wondered what reason God would have for allowing me this opportunity? How could I use this experience for God's glory, as Betty Cuthbert had done through her running?

As we returned home, I expected life to return to normal, but it wasn't to be. I had an article about me in the local paper, which included the torch relay, but also about my service to my local church. Anyone reading this article would know that I was a Christian. The Sunshine Coast Daily also interviewed myself, and another lady from the Sunshine Coast who had carried the torch too.

Next the local TV filmed and interviewed us at a school, as we were asked to share our experiences with the children. Dressed in my torch bearer tracksuit, I went to this school and, afterwards, was sitting having a coffee at the nearby shopping centre. I was aware of an elderly lady close by, who kept looking at me. Meanwhile the Lord was putting in my mind an idea of how I could witness to the Lord Jesus Christ by using the story of the torch relay. Then this lady began to talk to me, and it turned out she was a Christian lady. Together we talked about using my experiences to reach people for Christ. I had never met this lady before. It was as if God was confirming to me what I was to do.

I asked around the local churches and schools, and took my video of Melbourne to the Baptist church, and to my small Wesleyan Methodist church. I took the torch that had carried the flame for that brief 400 metres, and which had been purchased by Coca Cola for me to keep.

I shared, "The flame on this torch was passed on from one person to another, and it was meant to spread a message of peace and unite all nations under the Olympic flame at the Olympic games. I see it as being likened to the power of the Gospel message, which is to be passed on and to be spread throughout the world. The light of the world was the one light, Jesus Christ, who died to set us free from the law of sin and death. He gave Himself on that cross so we could live forever with Him. Each one of us, as

Christians, are to carry the light of Christ with us wherever we go, so that all men would know the love of God."

Matthew 5:14-16 says, *"You are the light of the world. A city that is set on a hill cannot be hidden. Nor do they light a lamp and put it under a basket, but on a lampstand, and it gives light to all who are in the house. Let your light so shine before men, that they may see your good works and glorify your Father in Heaven."*

I had the opportunity of sharing this message in a nearby public school and, as the principal was a Christian, she allowed me to speak about my Christian faith. I was next invited to speak to the 600 or so school children at the Christian college, and show them my torch. I spoke about how important it was to accept the Lord Jesus Christ as Saviour, as He is the light in this dark world.

I am aware that many Christians see the Olympics as a pagan ceremony, and I agree that its roots are from the pagan worship of the Roman Gods. Yet Paul used the illustration of running a race, which would have its roots in the ancient Olympic games. The runner runs his best to only attain a crown, such as a laurel wreath. In 1 Corinthians 9:24-25 it says, *"Do you not know that those who run in a race all run, but one receives the prize? Run in such a way that you may obtain it. And everyone who competes for the prize is temperate in all things. Now they do it to obtain a perishable crown, but we for an imperishable crown"* Paul is telling us that, as Christians, we must train ourselves and discipline ourselves to run the Christian race to the best of our ability! Our prize is eternal life, not just a laurel wreath.

I know the discipline that running and athletics take. Six of my eight children have done Little Athletics, which allows children and teenagers the chance to try all sorts of athletic disciplines. They all enjoyed their sport, and often competed at a regional and state level. My daughter, Sarah, was good at most athletic events, although later in life she would turn her attention more to dancing, especially through high school. Most of the children were good at middle distance running and, during the off season, would do cross country to keep fit.

One of my youngest sons, Ben, still trains and has competed at a national competition in decathlon, probably one of the toughest events. It involves all athletic disciplines, such as sprints, hurdles, middle distance, jumps, throws, and pole vault. You have to be training constantly, and have different specialist coaches to cover all the events. Ben was blessed in Australia to have two coaches, who were a husband-and-wife team from the Sunshine Coast. Both had represented Australia at an Olympic or Commonwealth level. His pole vault coach had also been a pole vaulter, and his wife a sprinter. They also have three children who all competed in sprints and pole vault. Their daughter has won Gold at the Commonwealth Games in pole vault, and was fourth at the recent Rio Olympics.

The reason I love watching my son compete is that I get to see all athletic disciplines, instead of just one, which is so much more interesting. It also makes me marvel, again, at the intricacies of the human body. As I watch Ben's graceful arching over the high jump bar, or the way his long legs can glide over 1 metre hurdles, it reminds me of what a great God we have in the way He created us. Psalm 139:13-14, *"For you formed my inward parts; you covered me in my mother's womb. I will praise you, for I am fearfully and wonderfully made."*

One of my favourite movies is 'Chariots of Fire', and most people would know the beginning scene as they run along the beach to Vangelis' music. I have walked along that beach at St Andrews in Scotland where it was filmed. I grew up a short way from St Andrews, and loved playing on that windy beach, where the famous home of the British Open golf tournament is across the road. I love the part where Eric Liddle, the Christian athlete, is explaining to his sister that once his studies, and the Olympic games, are over, he would be going to China as a missionary.

He says to her, "I love God, Jenny, and my desire is to serve Him, but He made me fast, and when I run, I can feel His pleasure!"

My son, Ben, was running one day, and listening to his Christian music, when he suddenly felt the presence of God very tangibly. He said he felt like Eric Liddell at that moment. God made us to run, dance, sing, and do it all to His glory!

PART TWO

PART TWO

Chapter 15

SARAH

The new house God had found for us was an older place, but it was also a little bit of paradise. Surrounded by bushland, and with lots of windows, it was lovely to see the sun shine through the trees, and have God's creation surrounding us. It was peaceful, and I was very thankful for God's provision. It would be our home for the next four years, and it was here that God would teach me how to fight in the Spiritual realm!

I had four children still at home. The twins, Joe and Ben, were in their last year of primary school, which was opposite where we lived. The girls, Sarah and Leah, were in high school, with Sarah in Year 11, and Leah in Year 9.

Sarah would struggle in the next few years, although it would not always be apparent. An extremely smart girl, with many gifts and talents, and with a personality which would strive to always want to be top of her class. Sarah would excel at sports, especially athletics, and was very driven to succeed in everything she did. To get an A was depressing for her, as she would expect to achieve an A+! Imagine trying to keep up with those sorts of self-imposed expectations.

One of the activities that kept Sarah going, and the one which would eclipse all others, was her love of dance. She loved to dance and, even though she had no formal dance training, seemed naturally gifted. When she was at primary school they had lip sync competitions, where you would make up a dance routine to one of your favourite pop songs, miming the words. Sarah was so good at putting together her dance routines, and lip syncing the words, that she frequently won. Her friends would get her to make up dances for them too. Sarah also got to be a backing dancer for an older girl, who was a singer. Sarah and two of her friends would do their dance routine while, Courtney took centre stage. Dance was a very important part of my daughter's life, that would bring her much joy, but also a measure of sorrow.

It was while living at Old Gympie Road that my daughter took the first overdose of painkilling tablets. It was a wakeup call for me that life was not going well for her. It was a confusing time for her as well. Although she was struggling emotionally, she still did well at school, sports, and dance. Communication was at an all-time low for us too, and I found it difficult getting my daughter to open up to me.

More alarm bells rang as I noticed, while cleaning her room one day, that there were cut out pictures of very skinny girls which she had pasted into a scrapbook. I was concerned, as they looked anorexic, and so it was that I realised that my daughter was not eating, or was eating very little. She could not afford to not eat as she was already slim, and did athletics and dance. The clothes she started wearing were unusually baggy to cover the fact that she was losing weight. I remember starting to serve dinner one night and, just as I put the plates out, she jumps up and says she is just going for a five-kilometre run, and would eat when she came back. This was a sign of anorexia, as eating would make an anorexic feel guilty, while exercise would make them feel better. In Psalm 107:18, the Bible says: *"Their soul abhorred all manner of food, and they drew near to the gates of death."*

To give hope to those who may be suffering from this eating disorder, in the next verse God says, *"Then they cried out to the Lord in their trouble, and He saved them out of their distresses. He sent His word and healed them, and delivered them from destructions."*

Anorexia is a silent killer which affects many teenage girls, and can also affect teenage boys too. Many people believe it is a modern-day illness, and blames the fashion industry which flaunt incredibly lean models as being the ideal body shape. Magazine ads, and teenage publications, showing unrealistic stereo types are also condemned for putting pressure on young girls. If you think it only affects those that are overweight, then think again. Anorexics don't see what they actually look like in the mirror. They see a distorted view of themselves and, instead, see a fat person, even when they aren't fat. It is also not entirely about body image, but also about the ability to control one's environment. When life seems out of control, for example pressure from school, work, or family, then controlling what you do and don't eat, is something the anorexic has some control over.

Looking at the causes of anorexia made my daughter one of the vulnerable ones. Experiencing loss or bereavement, being a perfectionist with a high achieving personality, and having a love of dance and athletics, both which demand a lean body was a disastrous combination. Another cause is depression and anxiety. Severe depression can cause a loss of appetite. In some instances, it can be a cry for help from sexual abuse.

As you can imagine, I was becoming anxious about what was happening in my daughter's life, and it was as if there were two of her. The beautiful girl, who went to church and did well at school. A young woman who danced beautifully and was talented at choreography. The other young woman who was secretive, hurting inside, taking pain killers, and starving herself. It was a confusing time for both of us and I didn't know what to do about it.

Parents if you see behaviour similar to what I have seen in my daughter, I would urge you to get help. Some signs of anorexia and self-harm can be:

- Not communicating – not wanting to talk about school, or what is happening in their life, to spending more time in their bedroom than with others in the family.
- Avoiding mealtimes – they always seem too busy to eat, and come home with a lunchbox full of food. They may also simply throw their lunch out, or give it away.
- Increase in the amount of exercise – always going for a run at strange times, especially meal times. Even when fit, they make excuses why they need to exercise more.
- Signs of depression – not eating, not sleeping well, poor communication, and having very little energy.
- Wearing baggy clothes to cover their weight loss.
- Obsession with pictures of skinny models, or magazines with pictures of very thin people.

The internet has sites where anorexics can get ideas, from other anorexics, on how to lose weight, and how to hide their weight loss. Bulimia is a condition where some binge eat, then feel guilty and make themselves vomit. Also remember that teenagers are often under a great deal of stress at school, especially in the last few years. It is important to not put extra pressure on them at this time.

Something which has been on the increase is self-harming. It can be taking painkillers, or cutting yourself with a knife. It is important to understand that emotional pain is far worse to these young men and woman, than physical pain. There are many causes, but some are caused by sexual, physical, or emotional abuse. Emotional abuse can be dealing with bullying, or constantly being told you won't amount to anything, or you're useless. When a teenager cuts themselves, they have a release of endorphins and, for a short amount of time, feel better. They will cover up sites where they cut. Wearing very unflattering clothing. Even on a hot day they will have long pants, and wear long sleeved shirts.

Chapter 16

WHERE TO GET HELP

I didn't quite know what to do and where to get help. As a Christian, I believe in prayer. I prayed, both by myself and with my pastor and his wife. As a Christian, it is very difficult to admit you are not coping with life, and I really didn't know who I could turn to. I knew the chaplain at the high school, and asked him if he knew what I could do about her anorexia and depression, but he wasn't a counsellor.

I then took her to a Christian counsellor who worked out of one of the churches. I waited outside while she talked to Sarah. I have no idea what was said, or if this counsellor wanted to see her again, but there was no attempt to speak to me, or recommend a further session. I have since worked as a nurse in a mental health unit, and the most frustrating thing for parents is the confidentiality between the psychologist or psychiatrist and the patient.

If it is your child and you are having to deal with suicidal tendencies, drug abuse, or self-harming, and don't know what is going on, you feel totally helpless. Teenagers are very good at manipulation, and making out everything is fine when in actual fact things are not fine. So, what do you do? The chaplain's wife, who was a friend of mine, found some information for me, and gave me some printouts about anorexia. It made me realise how serious this can be and, if not dealt with, could have life threatening consequences!

I knew of a Christian organisation up the coast that helped teenage girls with issues, such as anorexia and drug abuse, and contacted them. They told me that my daughter was not bad enough to need their help! Again, I thought how bad does it have to get? Do we wait until her liver or heart are irreparably damaged, or she commits suicide? I was frustrated, even when she took the pills I mentioned at the beginning of my story, as no follow-up was done by the mental health unit. All I could do was pray, and hope things got better. I continued to work part time, serve in my church, and try to look after my family the best way I could.

Chapter 17

A GLIMMER OF HOPE

It was 2005, which would be Sarah's final year in high school, and a year when my daughter would struggle and excel. The school captaincy was something a high achiever, such as my daughter, would covet as being one of the pinnacles of success at school. She had been the school captain at Beerwah Primary but, unfortunately, she did not get the votes she needed and would have to be content with being one of the prefects. As a prefect she would be expected to have exemplary behaviour, and this would be difficult as the emotional scars were still deep. There would be times when even remaining a prefect would be in doubt, as she would drink before the school disco and get in other sorts of trouble. I didn't really know what was happening most of the time because communication wasn't good and because a busy single mother's life could be overwhelming. A few of the teachers were concerned, and knew she was struggling. I think they stood up for her at times.

In Year 12, the stress levels and demands on the students are tremendous. They have major exams to sit, and an assessment which counts toward their OP scores, necessary in achieving that entry into university. If they get a high banding from 1 to 6 then they have more courses to choose from. The high achievers would strive to get a 1, as that would make you one of the top students in the state. There are only so many OP ones on offer.

Life would become very busy and stressful, but the one thing that kept Sarah going was her love of dancing. In all the subjects that Sarah would do, dance was her best. Keep in mind that my daughter had no formal training in dance, and no ballet, jazz or tap training. Another girl in her year level was also a very good dancer, and had done ballet for many years. Both girls would desire to have the top score, and hope to get the end of year award for dance.

Sarah had a gift for contemporary dance, whereas the other girl was good at ballet. Every second year, the high school would prepare for dance night. This is where all the dancers, from every year level, would perform, and tickets sold out fast for this type of event. Sarah would dance in many dances that night but, as a year 12 dance student, she would also be responsible for choreography of about seven dances for other groups. Again, this is a lot of pressure to be under, but it was the sort of challenge that Sarah loved. The night would be a special one, especially for me as I was so proud of her achievements despite the difficult times we had been through. Sarah, and the other girls in year 12 involved with dance night, would be in the local paper. It was a truly memorable night.

The other positive event that took place was that Sarah began to date the School Captain, a boy called Lewis. This happened half way through Year 12, and it made a big difference to Sarah's mental state. In September, the local chaplaincy committee raises money by putting on a debutante ball. Lewis' brother, Davis, was to be involved. It is a lovely, old-fashioned idea, and is a coming-of-age celebration. The young people have a partner whom they learn to dance with and they all get presented to the principal in their tuxedos and beautiful white dresses.

As Davis' brother, Lewis was allowed to bring someone to the dance. It was lovely to see Sarah all dressed up, and her handsome young man call by to pick her up. It was a special night for both of them. I remember when he walked through the door all dressed up, and Sarah looked so beautiful. They just seemed so right for each other. They would remain together to the end of Year 12 and, for those last months of high school, my daughter would be very happy.

The end of the year finally arrived, and the awards night was one of the main events of the year. Lewis was to be the 2005 Dux of the school, which is the highest academic achievement award, and he would also be the winner of the All-Round Male Student Award. Sarah would be the All-Round Female Student of the Year and, of course, the award which she coveted most would be the award for dance. She was not to be disappointed and, for a young girl who was without formal training, who started out at primary school winning lip sync competitions, it would be an amazing moment in finally achieving this coveted award.

She also achieved a very high achievement for dance, which was a VHA + (Very High Achievement). It was based on video tape of her dances, and also on her skills as a choreographer. The videos were reviewed by the Education department and she was awarded a VHA 8, or one of the highest achievements you can get for dance! With a final OP score of 6, she believed she would have no trouble getting into dance at university. At their formal, Sarah and Lewis would dance the night away, and everything looked like it was going to be just fine.

I wasn't to know what a bumpy ride we were all in for in the year ahead…

Chapter 18

DARK DAYS AHEAD

Sarah had applied to do performing arts in dance at the Queensland University of Technology. The crux of the application was an audition to show the dance department that you had what it took to be a dancer.

Lewis, Sarah, and myself went down to Brisbane for the auditions. It was a very hot summer's day, and Lewis and I spent a lot of time waiting and praying for Sarah. She gave her best, and was excited to hear what the outcome would be. This was her dream and deepest desire. Once she started her dancing the following year, it would help her to get through the disappointment of Lewis going to Brazil. He would spend a year in Sao Paulo as an exchange student, arranged by a community service club.

The day she got the letter to say she had not made the cut at the auditions was painfully devastating. Their reasoning was she had no ballet training, and they would not consider her under the circumstances. After her amazing result at high school, and her natural ability, they could not see past her lack of ballet training. If they had just given her a chance, she would have caught up with extra classes, but they were not prepared to take the chance. I had been told by an Eisteddfod judge that, if you didn't start ballet by the age of five or six, you would never be a ballerina. Sarah would prove them both wrong in the years ahead.

The time came to say goodbye to Lewis at Brisbane airport. It would be another painful disappointment. To lose her chance at a dance career and her boyfriend at the same time, brought all the emotional hurt back, and would crush her spirit once again.

Sarah was determined not to give up on her dream, and was also desperate to leave home and go out on her own. I wasn't so keen on this because of the concern over her anorexia and depression. I was pleased when she found a flat with two other Christian girls. We helped to move her into the flat where I thought she would be happy. She was able to find a job at Best and Less, a clothing store. Her sister, Esther, lived close by with her husband, Richard. She enrolled in ballet classes, and would keep her fitness up by jogging. I prayed that this would turn out to be a good year for Sarah, but it was very, very short lived.

Her sports teacher at the high school would keep in touch with Sarah, and whether my daughter confided in this teacher that she was struggling, I don't know. The teacher suggested to Sarah, without speaking to me, that there was a dance school up the coast that taught ballet and all other types of dancing. Well, this meant Sarah wanted to move home again after just two weeks! It was such a stressful time for me as it was a big job to move her to Brisbane in the first place. This particular dance school was not cheap either, and I struggled to find the money to allow her to go. Sarah gave up her job and, believing it would make her happy, we moved her back home. I thought if she gets to do what she loves every day, it will be worth it. I gave in to all the demands to let her begin full-time dance lessons. I prayed fervently to the Lord that this would help my daughter get her life back!

The dance school also taught tap dancing and singing. The students were encouraged to get work with musical productions to make money towards their lesson costs. Sarah had no interest in singing or tap. The students were all slim and good looking, and the ballet class had wall to wall mirrors. This began the fight, once more, with body image, constantly comparing herself to everyone else. After a few weeks of knowing I couldn't pick her up every day, I went out on a limb to borrow money for a new car for myself, and a car for her. I was concerned about her safety getting home at night. This was one of the biggest mistakes I have ever made, as that car was to give my daughter the freedom to live a lifestyle that would very quickly get out of control. It was clear, after a few weeks of going to this dance school, that Sarah was not happy. Sarah quit the dance school, which was a relief to me because the costs were so high! It was also not helping my daughter's mental state.

There was a spiritual fight going on inside my daughter. Having had a Christian upbringing, even giving her testimony in public that Jesus was her Saviour, did not end the struggles she was having. The pastor from our Wesleyan church had asked if anyone would like to be baptised. Sarah's sister, Leah, decided she wanted to be baptised, and Sarah decided she would be baptised too.

At the same time there was a lady who had come into our church who was an ex-drug addict on the methadone program. She would sit in church and fall asleep through the service. Pastor Lionel and his wife were very lovely people, and came alongside this lady, who had decided to give her life to Christ. She was to be baptised at the same time as my daughters. I later look back on this time, in the light of the spiritual battle that was to come, and believe the enemy had infiltrated our midst!

Matthew 7:15 says: *"Beware of false prophets who come in sheep's clothing, but inwardly they are ravenous wolves."*

It was a beautiful day in May when my daughters were baptised after church. It would take place at Ewan Maddock Dam. A lovely spot. Pastor Brendan would play his guitar, and we would sing our praise to God. As a mother, I was so excited to see my two youngest daughters go through the waters of Baptism. Pastor Lionel would baptise them, as well as the other lady. I welcome the fact that people are given the chance to repent and be baptised. This lady may have meant to follow Christ. I don't know. She continued taking methadone, which meant the need for drugs was still there. Was it just a coincidence that my hurting daughter Sarah was baptised with a drug addict? In four short months Sarah, herself, would be addicted to methamphetamines!

This same lady would almost break up my pastor's marriage. They took her into their home, and she would play one off against the other. My pastor and his wife, Jan, are the most loving and kind people. Their only desire is to show the love of Christ, and help people find Christ for themselves. Their son, David, is a pastor in the Solomon Islands. In the end they had to save their marriage and ask this lady to leave their home. It turned out it wasn't just drugs, but also witchcraft this lady was involved in.

"For we do not wrestle against flesh and blood, but against principalities, against powers, against the rulers of the darkness of this age, against spiritual hosts of wickedness in the heavenly places." (Ephesians 6:12)

Meanwhile Sarah had no work. I spoke to a Christian farmer we knew, who was the same man I worked for packing strawberries after Phil died. It was strawberry season once again, and Sarah got work planting, and then would get work picking when the fruit was ready. The other job Sarah did was for the local baker while she was at school. Her older brothers and sisters had worked there too. The couple who owned the bakery knew my children were hard workers and, as soon as one would go off to university, they would ask if any of my other children were old enough to work. Sarah was the last of my children to work there.

Unfortunately, they had hired a baker who liked the ladies. Sarah would start work at 6 am to slice the bread, and get the shop ready for the day's trade. Early in the morning she would be alone with this man, and he would stare at her and make rude comments, and he would come out for a look at every girl who came into the store. My daughter could usually handle herself well but, increasingly, became uncomfortable about his unwanted attention. On a Wednesday night she would play touch football at the local sports field. This baker would come down and stare at her while she was playing. He was a married man!

One day Sarah told me what was going on, and that she didn't feel comfortable working with this man. I approached the owners and told them what Sarah had told me. The owner's wife said she wasn't surprised, so I took it to mean they knew what he was like. The next time my daughter turned up for work on the Saturday, the owner told her he didn't believe she was being sexually harassed, and that this man was a good baker. (As if being a good baker meant he was trustworthy!) She worked that day with the owner's daughter, and had been crying because the owner had trusted the baker over her.

The daughter said to Sarah, "What's wrong with you? Did you have too much to drink last night?"

My daughter was so upset! That would be the last of my children to ever work there. I was so disappointed in their attitude. We have to protect our young people from this type of sexual harassment!

To begin with, the strawberry farm worked out, and then slowly changes became apparent in my daughter's behaviour. Moving out into a share house with a few friends from school, then smoking and drinking, and she was still only seventeen. The influence of the itinerant workers at the farm was rubbing off on Sarah. Her depression over her boyfriend being away, and not dancing, was also taking its toll. I believe it was at the strawberry farm that she would first try drugs. Sarah also decided to get her nose pierced. It was when she wanted to get a tattoo that I had to say something. Her father and I were not keen on our children having tattoos as they are permanent. If someone becomes a Christian, and has tattoos, then it is a new life they are starting. I would never judge anyone for this but, as a family, we wanted our children to consider the implications of having marks put on their bodies that are permanent. I also believe that those who do tattooing can be into witchcraft, and this can affect Christians spiritually.

Romans 12:1 says: *"I beseech you therefore, brethren, by the mercies of God, that you present your bodies a living sacrifice, holy and acceptable to God, which is your reasonable service."*

I remember writing a letter mentioning that her father would not have wanted her to get a tattoo. That letter stopped my daughter, and she has not had one to this day. What a difference a few months make – from baptism, to smoking, drinking alcohol, and living a lifestyle far removed from the one that, I believe, God had planned for her.

Chapter 19

LEARNING HOW TO FIGHT BACK!

During this time, Lewis and Sarah would communicate less and less. While he was away, I chose to keep in touch with him, still hoping Sarah would come back. Lewis was staying with a family in Sao Paulo, and they would go to the poorer parts of the city on a Friday evening and help feed the poor. Lewis also started attending a church for English-speaking people over there.

I prayed for him, as well as my daughter. I felt they were meant to be together, and it was hard to see them drifting apart. I felt increasingly helpless as to what I could do to bring my daughter back, and to help her. I decided that I needed to learn how to pray for her more effectively and asked God, "Please show me how to pray, Lord?"

The next week at church there were leaflets on the table by the door. The leaflets were about courses run by a group who practised, and taught, spiritual warfare. I immediately thanked God for his provision, as I believed this was an answer to my prayer! There would be about four sessions in the series, and they would be two weeks apart. I believe this was from the Lord, and I signed up for every one of them. As I soaked up the teaching on the battle for our minds, and how to fight in the spirit, I realised more and more how the enemy worked, and how to combat him. I could see the attacks on my daughter for what they were, attacks from the Enemy, and I was determined to fight back!

One of the important lessons I learned was to protect myself during the battle, which meant putting on the whole armour of God. It was critical to know the power in the name of Jesus, and also the power in the covering of the blood of Christ. To engage the enemy, when unprotected, is dangerous. A soldier would not dare go to battle unless he was trained, and had on the right battle gear. This group of prayer warriors showed me the importance of the armour.

Ephesians 6:10-13 says: *"Finally brethren be strong in the Lord and the power of His might. Put on the whole armour of God, that you may be able to stand against the wiles of the Devil. For we do not wrestle against flesh and blood, but against powers, against the rulers of the darkness of this age, against spiritual hosts of wickedness in the heavenly places. Therefore, take up the whole armour of God, that you may be able to withstand in the evil day, and having done all, to stand."*

I had to make a stand against the powers and rulers of darkness, and stand strong in the power of God. Daily I put on my armour, as it says in, Ephesians 6:14-18: *"Stand therefore, having girded your waist with truth, having put on the breastplate of righteousness, and having shod your feet with the preparation of the gospel of peace; above all taking the shield of faith with which you will be able to quench the fiery darts of the wicked one. And take the helmet of salvation, and the sword of the Spirit, which is the word of God; praying always with all prayer and supplication in the spirit, being watchful to this end with all perseverance and supplication for all the saints."*

To make it easier to remember the armour I would start with the top of my head. I would speak it out loud in the car or at home.

I would put on the helmet of salvation, and remember that through Christ I am saved!

I would then put on the breastplate of righteousness, for Christ is my righteousness and my own righteousness is as filthy rags.

Next was the belt of truth, which was a way of battling the wicked one when he sends his lies to you. Combat them with correct doctrine, and the truth found in the word of God.

Then would come the shoes of the gospel of peace. To be Christlike in all that I do. To be peace to all those around me.

The shield of faith is so important, to not allow the enemy a stronghold, and to believe in all the promises of God! To know you are on the Lord's side, as He is the light of the world.

John 1:5 says: *"And the light shines in the darkness, and the darkness did not comprehend it."* Darkness cannot overcome the light.

The sword of the spirit was to be used again and again, as I used God's word as a two-edged sword to battle the Devil's lies and condemnation.

I would cover myself with the blood of Christ, so that when God looks at me He sees the covering of the blood of His Son. When the Devil looks at me, he sees the payment for my sins in the blood of Christ, my Saviour.

It is also important to pray in the name of Jesus, as His name is powerful in the pulling down of strongholds.

Phil. 2:10-11 says: *"that, at the name of Jesus, every knee should bow, of those on earth, and of those under the earth, and that every tongue should confess that Jesus Christ is Lord, to the Glory of God the Father."*

How often do we remind the Devil about the power we have in the name of Jesus? I often just speak His name out loud, as it is a powerful weapon against the enemy. When we pray we make our petitions known to God, in the name of Jesus!

I also learned to negate the curses that we sometimes place on ourselves, and that others place on us. Curses like: 'I can never do that!' 'I am no good.' 'Who would care about me?' 'Life is too hard!' We need to repent of those negative words.

Psalm 19:14 says: *"Let the words of my mouth, and the meditation of my heart, be acceptable in your sight, O Lord, my strength and my Redeemer."*

Repent of words of self-condemnation, and replace them with the word of God.

I Corinthians 6:20 says: *"For you were bought at a price; therefore glorify God in your body and in your spirit which are God's."*

Curses also come against us simply because we are Christians. Those who simply don't understand the gospel, and also those who are against the gospel, will curse us. Satanists and witches curse us. We can negate the curses spoken over us, in Jesus' name. I found this out as I learned spiritual warfare, and attended a prayer group that prayed against the spiritual forces of darkness. Witches prayed against us and, in the middle of fighting for my daughter, a visiting Christian speaker came to our town. He was known to have a prophetic gift, and was giving many positive, encouraging messages, until he came to pray for me. He said, "there are witches praying against you!"

Well, thanks very much I thought. I knew I had engaged the enemy, and they were not going to win. I simply said out loud, "I negate all curses coming against me from witchcraft, in Jesus' name." There is power in the name of Jesus!

It was with the warfare group that I also had personal ministry. One of the ladies who ran this particular ministry, was given a gift of seeing in the spirit, while her husband would pray for whatever was seen and needing dealt with. Whether a Christian or not, there are still spiritual forces influencing us, especially when we engage the enemy. Monday nights was the night for warfare prayer and, inevitably when it was time to go, I would be overcome with fatigue. If I allowed this to influence me, I would stay home but, if I fought through it, I would go to the prayer meeting and have plenty of energy. The enemy does not want to engage us, so they will try to oppress us instead.

One day, I was at home in bed when I woke up in the middle of the night with left-sided chest pain. It was very frightening, as I am a cardiac nurse and know only too well the signs of a heart attack. I prayed out to God, and was sitting in the lounge room not knowing whether to go to hospital or wait. My son, Joe, heard me, and got up and prayed for me. Then his twin brother, Ben, got up, and I told the boys I needed to go to hospital. Ben drove me, and all the way to hospital I had excruciating pain. I thought that maybe this was it, and I wouldn't make it!

I arrived at the emergency department and they hooked me up to a monitor, and I was given morphine for the pain. They took blood tests, and also a special test to discount if I had a pulmonary embolism (a blood clot in the lung). Everything was clear, and the pain left me. I went home much relieved. The next night a similar thing occurred, and I woke up with chest pain again. This time I stood my ground, and rebuked Satan, and bound the spirit of pain in my chest. It suddenly left, and I was able to go back to sleep. I was recounting the story to a friend at church, and he told me that two other people had experienced the same thing that week from our church. Christians we can, and do, come under attack spiritually.

It was while I was with this warfare group that I continued to learn to fight in the spirit for my daughter. Sarah had decided she wanted to go to Bundaberg, four hours' drive north from us. Apparently, there was more farm work up there. I was concerned about her going so far away, especially as I realised the seasonal pickers were not a good crowd to be around. Sarah insisted on leaving, and went with a friend from school whom I knew would watch over her.

Meanwhile I continued to pray, go to work, and look after the three children still at home.

Chapter 20

I MEET TIM

Sarah hadn't been gone long when I received a phone call from Bundaberg.

"Hello, Mrs Brown. This is Tim, here, the supervisor at the tomato farm. Your daughter Sarah has had an accident with the ladder used to pick tomatoes and, as she was climbing down the ladder, slipped and caught her finger in the hinge of the ladder. I drove her to the hospital as her finger is badly hurt. But she's okay, and is just having her finger bandaged in emergency."

I replied, "Thank you for taking care of her, and getting her to the hospital. Please have her call me when she can."

I got off the phone, wondering what else could go wrong in Sarah's life, and who was this Tim? He seemed very gallant and charming on the phone, and I would soon meet him face-to-face. I never dreamed that a phone call from this young man would be the beginning of a journey which would bring a lot of pain and heartache. Tim would take my daughter further and further from God's plan for her life.

Sarah was to celebrate her 18th birthday in a couple of months, and we were to meet with the rest of the family at a Chinese restaurant near where we lived. Sarah was going to drive down from Bundaberg and stay over. I waited all day for her to come, knowing that family were coming from Brisbane to see her. Nervously I waited, and waited, wondering if she would ever make it! Eventually she arrived at the house, just before we were to go out, but she was not alone. The man called Tim, who had been so helpful when Sarah had hurt her finger in the picking ladder, had also come home with her. I had been looking forward to having my daughter home, knowing she was safe under my roof. Instead she had brought a young man home whom I knew nothing about.

Sarah looked shy and not herself.

"Hi, Sarah. It's so good to see you," I exclaimed, as I hugged my daughter. I could smell cigarette smoke on her clothes as we hugged. Turning, I looked at the young man who was standing nearby with his shoulders hunched, staring at the floor.

"Mum, this is Tim," Sarah blurted out. "The man who spoke to you on the phone from the hospital."

"It's nice to meet you, Tim. I'm very grateful for you looking after my daughter when she had her accident."

He continued to look at the floor, as he mumbled a reply, "That's okay. It's my job to look after the workers."

Sarah looked very uncomfortable, as if she didn't want to be there.

Tim said goodbye, and left in Sarah's car. I quickly drove us to the restaurant, where the family had been patiently waiting for us. It was the most awkward meal, as my daughter hardly spoke, but kept checking her phone messages and going outside to smoke. I felt confused and just wanted us all to enjoy her 18th birthday. The family didn't know what to say as we waited for our meals. All the time she was messaging Tim about when he could pick her up, and they could go and party. I was beginning to wonder if this girl could possibly be my daughter, so much had changed in the few months since Lewis had left.

Sarah said, "Thanks for the dinner everyone and the presents, but I really have to go. My boyfriend's waiting for me outside."

Her boyfriend? Since when, I thought. What was going on, and how could she have another boyfriend? In a few short months Lewis would be home, and I was sure they would get back together! Surely this was a mistake!

"Sarah, the family have driven all the way from Brisbane. And you're going?"

"Tim's waiting, Mum. I have to go!"

"I thought you were staying at home tonight!"

"There's a party up the coast, and we're going. So I won't be home tonight, and we're leaving for Bundaberg tomorrow."

Tim met her in the car park outside, with Sarah's car, a car I wish I had never purchased. It was meant to keep her safe, not to pursue a dangerous way of life! They left, and I wasn't to see Sarah again for many months.

At this time of year, the warfare prayer team I was a part of would gather down in Victoria, for a week of prayer for the nation. This was in November 2006, and my friend, Heather, and I decided to join the team. One thing I believe the Devil loves to do is interfere with our walk with God, and disrupt any task that God might set us. He will use our emotions, our families and any other means to distract us from our purpose in Christ. God had called me to pray and intercede for the nation, and those He would bring into my life. I continued to pray for Sarah, but I was also determined not to be put off doing what God had called me to do! I also believed that, after Sarah's disappointing birthday reunion, I was badly in need of a distraction!

We flew to Melbourne, and met another couple from Queensland who we would pray with that week. From Melbourne, we drove a hire car down to the south of the state. It was summer in Australia, but the place in Victoria we were going to is down on the Tasman Sea. I was not prepared for the weather being so cold. The couple who ran the ministry had a farm and raised sheep, as well as running their ministry. They had a few hotel-type units guests could stay in for the prayer week.

The week was amazing, as we had fellowship and prayed together. The food was wonderful too, especially the Aussie lamb straight from the farm! We also had time for some sightseeing, and went up into the mountains and nearby towns. While in Victoria I was getting emails from the telephone company about a bill for telephone charges for my daughter's mobile phone. They were up to $200 a month! I had made the mistake of co-signing my daughter's mobile phone plan. Because she was only 17 when she got the phone, I had to go guarantor for the repayments. That was a decision which would be very costly, and I would urge parents not to make the same mistake. When I checked the charges, they didn't make sense. It was one more reason I was extremely concerned at what was happening with Sarah.

Chapter 21

REALISATION DAWNS

I returned back to the Sunshine Coast and tried to talk to my daughter. I kept messaging her to find out about the phone bills. It was the end of the year, and my children, Leah, Ben, and Joe, were at one of their athletics' carnivals. It was special for me to watch my children compete. As I sat on the hill watching the events, and cheering the children on, I received a text message. It was short and to the point. It was from Sarah, and it read, "I am a drug addict, Mum."

I sat there dazed on that beautiful summer day absolutely stunned and disbelieving! This message was not telling me that she was smoking cannabis, this was a message letting me know she was hooked on methamphetamines, which would explain the crazy phone bills I'd been getting! What was I going to do? In that moment I thought it was beyond my comprehension, as I never imagined one of my children could possibly be an addict!

I knew in my heart that things were not right, so it wasn't a complete surprise. I am grateful that Sarah told me the truth. She could have tried to cover it up, but she didn't and, for that, I am grateful. I now knew the enemy, and what I was fighting against. To be effective in prayer, I believe that we need to target the spirits involved.

My daughter, Esther, knew a couple whose son had an addiction problem. The addiction to drugs became an addiction to alcohol, and I rang the father and asked for advice. The answer he gave me was to look after myself, and try not to worry. I just could not do that! My daughter's life, and her soul, was in danger. I made up my mind that I would use every manner of warfare God would show me. I would pray without ceasing and battle the *"...rulers of the darkness of this age."* (Eph. 6:11)

I would not take them on alone, however. To do that would not be wise. I continued to go to my warfare prayer meetings, and learn to fight in the spirit. I prayed as often as I could with my pastor, and others at my church. The warfare group also prayed, as did the couple who ran the ministry in Victoria. I would meet with my special friend, Heather, from the Baptist church, and whomever else was willing to pray with me.

One practical thing I did was to go to Bundaberg, and try to speak to my daughter face-to-face. I hoped that she would want to come home once she had seen me. My eldest son, Aaron, said he would come with me. He would have loved to have confronted her boyfriend, Tim, as he believed him to be the cause of Sarah's drug habit. It was a four-hour drive.

I rang Sarah and said, "Sarah I need to talk to you about this drug habit. And I need to know you're okay."

I don't think she was very keen, but she replied, "If you want, Mum. We could meet at a cafe at the shopping centre. Message me when you get here."

I arrived early, and sat with my son, gazing around at the shoppers going by, wondering if they knew that my daughter was addicted to meth. Well, of course they didn't, but it felt so unreal, and my nerves were beginning to get the better of me. Doubts then began as I wondered if she would show up at all.

"Aaron what if we have come all this way and she doesn't show up?"

"Don't worry, Mum. She'll be here soon. I wish that good-for-nothing Tim would come too, so I could give him a walloping!"

It seemed forever we had been waiting and, when she finally arrived, it was a relief. I was so nervous because I didn't quite know what to expect.

"Sarah," I exclaimed, as I grabbed her and hugged her tight.

As soon as we pulled apart, I realised with shock that she had changed since we had last seen each other. She had always been slim, but now she was painfully thin, and looked agitated.

Methamphetamines are sometimes known as 'Speed' because they speed up the metabolism and give you more heightened senses. It's like over-revving a car engine. It may feel good, but the damage it does to the body is dangerous. After the high comes the low, when the drug wears off, the body crashes, and the user wants to sleep. The cycle then begins again, with the body craving the drug to again feel that euphoric sensation. It gives a heightened sense of pleasure, but at a dreadful cost. For someone who struggles with body image, it also keeps you thin, giving Sarah an added reason to use the drug. The emotional pain Sarah felt would also be diminished for a time, but the cause of the pain would remain.

The other down-side of drug use, besides the obvious detriment to the body, is that you lose all sense of what is right and wrong. The need for the fix is so overwhelming that you will do anything for it! Because it costs to buy the drugs, you spend most of your government payments on it. This leads to owing people money, such as drug dealers, stealing, and doing things that you would never think of doing otherwise.

It was so good to see her, but heart-wrenching having to say goodbye again.

"Sarah, how are you doing?" I asked.

"I'm fine, Mum. Really I am."

"I'm worried about you. This is no place for a young girl, Sarah. You have your whole life in front of you. We can get you help to come off the drugs. Please come home with your brother and I!"

"Mum, I'm happy here with Tim, and I don't want to come home. You need to understand that this is my life!"

She would not come home, and we could not force her, unless we kidnapped her. The drugs, and Tim, were to keep her from coming home for over a year. One positive thing was that Tim's mother and step-father were concerned for Sarah, and tried to encourage her to go home. They even gave her money for petrol, but they would just spend it on more drugs.

Driving home was sad, and I felt very empty. I was glad of my eldest son's company. I needed to not lose heart, but instead to become more determined in my prayer life.

I decided to go online, and see if there were any organisations who could help me. I knew about Teen Challenge in the city of Toowoomba, but they were only catering for men. Teen Challenge has a great program, and a really good success rate for those who are motivated to get help for their addiction. Unfortunately, there is discipline involved, and you have to go completely without drugs, alcohol, and cigarettes once you step in the house. This can be so hard for people, especially an adult male who is used to his own way. It is not a question of a lack of help being available, but in motivating the person to freely enter a program. This is where spiritual warfare comes into the equation.

Another place I asked for help was Drug Arm. They are an organisation involved in educating people on the dangers of recreational drug use. It certainly opens your eyes when you learn the reasons behind people using these drugs, and how they can so easily become addicted. It also gives you information on how they work in the body, and the sensations people experience from their use. They explain what the side effects are – anything from increased heart rate, to weight loss, overdose, and death. It is extremely scary if you have a family member you love taking these substances.

It is interesting to note that my husband had decided, the year I was pregnant with Leah, my sixth child, to start a market in the neighbouring town of Landsborough. I remember that, on one particular market day, he invited Drug Arm to display their information on drug abuse, and the different drugs people become addicted to. Sarah then was only around 16 months old and, at the time, I never paid much attention to the display!

I found out where Drug Arm was located, which was in Brisbane near the Royal Brisbane Hospital. I rang them, and made an appointment to speak with their counselling team. I remember it was a very hot day, and I got off the train at the closest rail station to their offices. Despite this, I wandered round unable to find them. Time was fast approaching when my appointment was due, and I ended up walking right round the block and finally found them on the corner. I had almost given up, and nearly went home feeling discouraged. But, praise God, I made the appointment.

"It's good to meet you, Mrs Brown. Please come in and sit down."

I sat down as two Drug Arm counsellors spoke to me.

"Please tell us about your daughter, and the circumstances of her addiction."

They listened intently as I explained about Sarah's life, up until she confessed her drug use. The loss of her father, the depression, self-harm, and anorexia she had struggled with, the meeting with Lewis at the high school, then the disappointments when he left to go overseas and her failed dance audition.

"So, Mrs Brown. We are very sorry for the dilemma you find yourself in. Have you thought of ways you could get your daughter to come home?"

"Well, that's why I'm here. To get advice from you!"

"What have you tried so far?"

"I went with my son to Bundaberg, to try to talk some sense to her, and that she was destroying her life and her health. But she wouldn't listen. There is a young man she has met, and he has a history of drug use which I was unaware of. He's older than Sarah. His mum and step dad said that Tim was unreliable, and impulsive, and had been on and off meth for years! What else can I do?"

Again they asked me what I could do to help bring her home. The only thing I could think of was the car. A car, which I had bought to keep my daughter safe, was now being driven around Bundaberg, and helping them have access to the drugs. It was a car I was paying for, and which was partly registered to me! This was a difficult dilemma to face because I worried that, without the car, Sarah would get into more trouble. It would mean her being stranded in Bundaberg, and becoming more dependent on people who could cause her harm.

"The car they drive is one I am paying for, and I've thought about taking it away from them."

"Perhaps that would be a good idea, as it might make your daughter think about her situation," they said.

I left Drug Arm with just as much discouragement as when I got there. I did have more information on the drugs that Sarah was using, but was now left with a very difficult decision to make concerning what I was to do about the car?

Chapter 22

THE STRONG MAN

I believe I did what I could in the natural realm. I knew where my daughter could get help, but I could not make the decision myself for her to receive that help. It is like telling someone about the Gospel, that Christ died for them and they can experience a new life. Knowing the story of Christ's death on the cross is not the same as accepting that He died for you, and making the decision to invite Him into your heart. It is the same as trying to convince an alcoholic he would be better without alcohol, but unless he is determined to do something about it, he will remain an alcoholic. This is where the person's will becomes important, as they need to be convinced that their lifestyle is unhealthy, and they need to change.

The lady who runs Oz Challenge with her husband, tells of the time when she worked for Teen Challenge in one of the major Australian cities. They would go out and talk to the prostitutes, buy them coffee or something to eat, and talk to them about Christ. Many would give their hearts to the Lord. As much as the prostitute who accepted Christ wanted to change her life, it was too hard, and most would resume their old lifestyle.

This lady came to the conclusion that there are spiritual forces at play that influence people's decision to continue down the wrong path.

People have different experiences of life. Some are brought up to only know love and acceptance. They may be brought up in the church, nurtured, given love at home, and never know poverty or abuse. Others may be brought up in a home where they are abused emotionally, physically, or sexually. It may be they are neglected in some way, and are not given the necessities of life. They may be from a single parent home, never knowing who their father is, or they may have an abusive step-parent. It can also be that they have endured a traumatic experience, such as rape or assault, possibly a car accident that has left them physically and emotionally damaged.

Imagine that your spirit has been damaged in some way. What happens in the spiritual realm is that the spirits of the wicked one see that our spirit is damaged, and a spirit is able to enter through the damaged area in that person's life. God is made up of three persons. God the Father, God the Son and God the Holy Spirit. We are made in God's image, and are also made up of three parts. The body, the soul (which is our personality), and our Spirit.

Romans 8:16 tells us that, *"The Spirit Himself bears witness with our spirit that we are children of God."* Therefore, God communicates with us through our spirit. It is only through the spirit of God that we can be saved. In John 3:5-6 Jesus says: *"Most assuredly, I say to you, unless one is born of water and the Spirit, he cannot enter the kingdom of God. That which is born of the flesh is flesh, and that which is born of the spirit is spirit."* Now what happens when the spirit becomes damaged, or broken, through abuse or trauma? The enemy takes advantage of our weakness, and sin enters this portal, separating us from God. I realise that this subject is contentious, but I am not coming from a place of reasoning or conjecture, but from a place of experience.

You might believe that spiritual forces cannot affect you as a Christian. James 4:1 says, *"Beloved, do not believe every spirit, but test the spirits, whether they are of God; because many false prophets have gone out into the world."* Is this verse talking about physical beings going out into the world, or spirits of false prophets? We know that men are used of the spirits of wickedness, but here it is talking about the lies and spiritual deception that is sent out. I have read of many famous Christians who have battled depression, or have been affected in their Christian lives from trauma. Remember, we will have tribulation, and we are at war. We may belong to Christ but, if our faith is under attack, or not strong, or we are new in the faith, we will be more likely to believe the lies that the enemy can use, and bombard us with. Spiritual deception is very real and, if we allow the thoughts of the devil to remain in our minds, then the stronghold grows and can be difficult to move.

It amazes me the stories I hear from the mission field in Africa, and other nations, where they believe very strongly in the spirit world and are in very real bondage, living in fear of what the spirits can do. When people hear the Gospel, they welcome the Holy Spirit because they know the spirit world is real. So many more people in third world countries are healed of diseases, blindness, and spiritual oppression, because they accept that this is part of being a Christian, and that the Holy Spirit is so much stronger than those they have dealt with.

I stayed at an Airbnb where the lady practised Hinduism and had shrines and a meditation room in the house. I stayed there while she was in India, staying at an Ashram. When she was leaving, she told me that everything should be fine and, if I had trouble with the boiler, there was a number I could ring.

She said, "I shouldn't have any problems." She then added, "But, there is another spirit in the house now."

You see she knew I was a Christian, and that the spirit that is in me is different from the spirit that is in her. In the spirit there was a conflict of interest. I did wonder how I came to be there…

I was reminded to put on the armour from Ephesians 6. I covered myself in the blood of Christ daily, and bound all the spirits not of God, sent them to the pit, and loosed into the house the Holy Spirit.

I declared, *"Greater is he that is in me then he that is in the world."* Nothing went wrong and I slept reasonably well. I had no problem with binding the spirits that were not of God. For God himself gave us the power to do this.

In Matthew 18:18 the word says, *"Assuredly, I say to you, whatever you bind on Earth will be bound in Heaven and whatever you loose on Earth will be loosed in Heaven."* This is also in Matthew 16:19, where Jesus is talking to Peter, and says, *"And I will give you the keys of the Kingdom of Heaven, and whatever you bind on Earth will be bound in Heaven, and whatsoever you loose on* Earth *will be loosed in Heaven."*

What is Jesus referring to in this passage? He is not telling his disciples to go around physically binding people with chains. He is not telling them to take off physical chains, but is referring to the inward chains that bind us, the spiritual powers that can become strongholds in our lives. Gods desire is that we fully make him our stronghold.

In Psalm 18:2 we read, *"My God, my strength, in whom I will trust; My shield and the horn of my salvation, my stronghold."* Stronghold is a word reflecting what controls us. If God is our stronghold, then we are under His control, which is what we desire most of all as we walk the Christian walk of faith. What can replace, or weaken, this stronghold is when other things have control of us, and they weaken our stronghold in Christ.

In Luke, Jesus gives us an illustration of a strong man. Jesus is again confronting the Scribes and Pharisees because he has cast out a mute spirit.

THE STRONG MAN

He is accused of doing it with the power of Beelzebub. Beelzebub is a ruling spirit. He tells them it is impossible for Satan to cast out Satan because his kingdom would collapse.

Then, in verses 21-22, He says this, *"When a strong man, fully armed, guards his own palace, his goods are in peace. But when a man stronger than he comes upon him, and overcomes him, he takes from him all his armour in which he trusted, and divides his spoils."* In this illustration Jesus is saying that the spirits are subject to Him because his Spirit is stronger than theirs. His Strong man is stronger than their strong man, therefore the strongholds that control us through sin, deception, or trauma, are subject to the strong man of the Holy Spirit.

In the next few verses Jesus, talks more specifically about the spiritual world.

Luke 11:24-26 says, *"When an unclean spirit goes out of a man, he goes through dry places, seeking rest; and finding none, he says, 'I will return to my house from which I came.' And when he comes, he finds it swept and put in order. Then he goes and takes with him seven other spirits more wicked than himself, and they enter and dwell there; and the last state of that man is worse than the first."*

The passage in Luke has gone from talking about a strong man to talking about unclean spirits. Both illustrations refer to a house or dwelling. Our bodies are the temple of the Holy Spirit. The Spirit dwells in us. Imagine that hurt, and grief, have overwhelmed you, like it did my daughter. A spirit of grief affects her. As time goes on, she goes to church, tries to live the Christian lifestyle, but the grief does not go away. The hurt remains and, when she is rejected by the university, and her boyfriend leaves her, the spirit of grief then says to the spirit of rejection, come and join me, and the spirit of addiction which is there at the lake where my daughters are to be baptised says, "Well why don't we join the spirits of grief and rejection."

These are all spirits of control that seek to separate us from the love of God, and make it difficult for the Holy Spirit to enter our home or temple. This is why being filled with the Holy Spirit is so important. Not only was Sarah contending with a spirit of grief, but also spirits of depression, anorexia, rejection, addiction and, the biggest one of all, deception. Deception is the one that makes all the rest seem more justified.

In Isaiah 44:20 it says, *"A deceived heart has turned him aside; and he cannot deliver his soul."*

In John 8:43-44, Jesus again confronts the scribes and Pharisees. He tells them, *"Why do you not understand My speech? Because you are not able to listen to My word."*

Why could they not understand the words of Jesus? He goes on to tell them: *"You are of your father the Devil and the works of your Father you will do. He was a murderer from the beginning, and does not stand in the truth, because there is no truth in him. When he speaks a lie, he speaks from his own resources, for he is the father of it."* They could not see the truth because they were blinded by a Spirit of deception. Where does it come from? It comes from the Devil.

In verse 47 Jesus says, *"He who is of God hears God's words; therefore you do not hear, because you are not of God."*

To overcome the strong man, or the spirit of deception, we must first bind the strong man, or render him powerless and replace the strongman with the spirit of God. He is greater than the strong man. Everyone knows what happens when you have a vacuum. As a nurse, I had a trick in drawing up medication into a syringe. If the syringe was empty, and I tried to draw up my drug, it would meet with resistance. If I drew air into the syringe, then put the needle into the vial and pushed that air into the solution, emptying the air out of the syringe, the solution would seek to fill the vacuum where the air had been, and my syringe would fill up without me having to make any effort. It is the same with our body, the temple of God. When we continually invite the Holy spirit in to fill us, there is no room for any other spirit to inhabit our house.

If we harbour a spirit of deception or grief, then we have an open door to other spirits to come in. Through Oz Challenge, I learned about these spirits of control that seek to disrupt our spiritual walk. One of the warfare tactics I was taught was to bind the spirits of control in my daughter. Many people become concerned at the use of the word 'spirit'. It is simply a way of explaining those things that the enemy of our souls uses to interfere with Gods' rule in our lives, and which inhibits the working of the Spirit of God.

For example, I would start by binding the spirit of anti-Christ. The anti-Christ spirit is that part of us that wages war against Christ. Next, I would bind the spirit of deception, then all the other spirits – such as depression, anorexia, addiction (naming those specific addictions), rejection, rebellion, and death. I would bind them with unbreakable chains, and send them to the pit where the Devil and his angels will go at the end of the age.

In Revelation 20:1-3 we see the binding of Satan by an angel. *"Then I saw an angel coming down from Heaven, having the key to the bottomless pit, and a great chain in his hand. He laid hold of the Dragon, that serpent of old, who is the Devil and Satan, and bound him for a thousand years; and cast him into the bottomless pit, and shut him up, and set a seal on him, so that he should deceive the nations no more till the thousand years were finished."* Here we have an example of binding the Devil himself, and notice it says, *"so that he should deceive the nations no more..."*

I then would loose into my daughter, replacing the spirits of control, with God's Holy spirit, and the fruits of Gods spirit of truth, love, joy, hope, peace, desire for healing, life, and salvation. Other ministries may have a different way of doing this. I am not saying other ways of praying don't work, but only relating one way of praying which, I believe, God showed me through Oz Challenge, and the word of God.

As I mentioned before, this lady from Oz Challenge had a gift of seeing in the spirit. When ministering to someone, God would show her the spirits controlling the person, and her husband would bind them and send them to the pit. Trudy could then see the spirits going to the pit. The spirits would then be replaced with Gods' spirit, and those fruits that come by the spirit of God. If the person was not a Christian, then they would pray for their eyes to be open to the saving grace of God. Spiritual deception works on the mind. That is where the attacks come. The negative messages that assault us.

Messages that tell us: 'You are unworthy to have God love you'; 'You know you need this drug to make you happy'; 'Why don't you just end it all right now'; or 'I must have deserved that!'

When the child of a Christian parent goes astray, it goes like this: 'God must not love you'; or 'You know you were selfish, and didn't look after your child'; or 'What sort of witness is that!'

I know only too well the lies the Devil can spin. I refused to listen, and decided to fight instead. Every day I would cover and bind the spirits of control over my daughter. The covering was the blood of Jesus. Daily I would cover and bind the spirits of the anti-Christ – rebellion, and rejection, addiction – and anything else that the Holy Spirit would show me, and then I would send them to the pit. I would then loose into Sarah, God's Spirit of truth, His love, a spirit of salvation, and freedom from drugs. This was strategy number one.

I expect there are those who doubt that this works, and I will give simple examples in my own life where God showed me that it does, indeed, work. I have an amazing mother, and I am very thankful to God for her. It became clear to me that, at times, my mother would bring up episodes that happened in the past, where she perceived people had hurt her. It was often my father who would bear the brunt of this. I felt my mother was dealing with a spirit of unforgiveness. I was not judging my mother, but only desired to see my parents happy and loving one another. I decided to pray for my mum by binding and covering the spirit of unforgiveness in her. I sent it to the pit and, instead, loosed into her a spirit of forgiveness. I never thought about it again until a few days later, and my mother rang me on the phone. This in itself was unusual, because she usually waits for me to ring her.

I asked how she was, and then she proceeded to say, "I was walking past the church on the corner on the way to the shops, and decided to go in and sit down. As I sat there, I felt God tell me that I needed to forgive others who had hurt me."

I was stunned by this admission because, as much as my mum loves and confides in me, I had never heard her admit any shortcoming to me before. Why did she ring me and reveal this revelation? I can only believe that the Holy Spirit was showing me confirmation that, how I was praying for my daughter, was real and effective.

I was to learn this at work too. A patient we were looking after had extensive leg ulcers that needed dressing every day. It wasn't a pleasant job, because it took time, and the patient was not the easiest to get along with. He often swore at us, and grumbled when we tried to get him into bed to do his dressings. I could see that the other nurses were reluctant to do the dressings, and so I volunteered.

I prepared the dressing trolley, and then felt the need to pray for the situation. I went into the staff toilet to pray.

"I bind the spirit of anti-Christ, blasphemy, non-cooperation, and unpleasantness in this patient."

I then decided I would be cheerful when going into his room, and to ask if he would mind getting into bed so I could dress his legs. He preferred to sit in the chair, and was usually reluctant to lie on the bed.

As I walked into the room, I discovered he was already on the bed, even though he had been sitting in the chair a moment before.

I politely asked, "Would you mind if I do your dressings on your legs now?"

"Sure. Go ahead," he replied, in a very civil manner. Surprised, we ended up having a very pleasant conversation.

The next thing that happened really startled me. He said, "It is time I went back to church."

I can't even remember what I said in response, but I think I was rendered speechless!

I am mindful when, at work, to remember that I am a nurse, and I have a responsibility to do my job well. Those I work with know I am a Christian, and there have been Christian nurses I have worked with. This has been such a blessing. I feel prompted by the Holy Spirit at times to pray for certain people, or I may have a quiet moment where I will ask if someone would like prayer. If they are a Christian, I can talk to them about the Lord, and pray for them. I am careful to not overstep my role at work. It doesn't mean I cannot be used by God though.

I had a lady who was very sick with a respiratory disease, and was battling to breathe. All her respiratory muscles were being used to suck in enough oxygen to keep her going. Despite the nebulisers and antibiotics we gave her, she struggled for every breath. I felt so helpless about what else to do, and so I went into the treatment room, which was empty, and spoke to the Lord.

"I bind you, spirit of respiratory distress, and the spirit of infirmity, and I send you both to the pit. I loose the Holy Spirit into her, and the healing power of the blood of Christ."

If you are an asthmatic, you will know what it is like when you have an asthma attack. It is exhausting and scary. I waited 5-10 minutes, and then went into her room. Immediately I sensed that she seemed different. I resisted asking her how she was. I wanted her to tell me if she felt better.

This lady looked at me and said, "It is the first time I have felt so well since I came into hospital."

Her breathing had settled almost immediately, and she was even able to get up after a while and walk down the corridor.

A friend I was working with commented, "Isn't it amazing that she can walk now, even though she could hardly breathe."

My friend isn't a Christian, but she knows I am, and I said that I had just prayed for her. God deserves the glory!

Chapter 23

WEAPONS OF OUR WARFARE – PRAYER

2 Corinthians 10:4 says, *"For the weapons of our warfare are not carnal, but mighty in God for pulling down strongholds."* What are the weapons of our warfare? One of the most important is prayer.

I will discuss the different aspects of prayer and how I used them to help bring down the strongholds in my daughter's life.

1. It is important when taking on the role of a prayer warrior that we are right with God. If we are living in disobedience to the word, and not walking in righteousness before God, then our prayers for others are less likely to be effective. Everyone struggles with sin, and we all need to come before the throne of Grace to ask for forgiveness and cleansing. There is only one that is perfect, and that is Christ, so when we come before Him, the Bible says in 1 John 1:9, *"If we confess our sins, He is faithful and just to forgive us our sins, and to cleanse us from all unrighteousness."*

2. In James 5:16 it says, *"...the effective, fervent prayer of a righteous man avails much."* Here we have the word fervent. So not only is righteousness a requirement, but being fervent in our prayers is important. This is the way Jesus prayed in Luke 22:44, *"And being in agony, He prayed more earnestly..."* Imagine you were told your daughter was on drugs, and you wanted to pray, would you pray earnestly or would you simply recite a nice prayer you'd heard? Somehow, I think you would be pleading before God for mercy for your daughter. When the problem is close at hand, and personal, it becomes more urgent. It should not necessarily be this way. All our prayers should be urgent, no matter who or what they are for, but the more personal the prayer, the more we will travail. Elijah was an effective prayer warrior and it says, *"Elijah was a man with a nature like ours, and he prayed earnestly that it would not rain, and it did not rain in the land for three years and six months."* In James 5:17, the Bible says he was just like us, yet his prayer stopped it raining for three and a half years!

3. Do we believe in prayer, and what prayer can achieve, or do we doubt and simply go through the motions? It is so important to pray believing that our prayers will be answered. If we are praying for God's will, then there should be no doubt that God will answer our fervent prayer. What makes intercessory prayer effective is that it is praying for needs outside of ourselves. To pray for someone else's need is powerful, and unselfish. Praying for my daughter was threefold. I wanted my daughter home so, in fact, it was selfish because I love her. Secondly, I wanted the best for her, which was to know God and to have a happy fruitful life. The third reason was to defeat the plan the enemy had for my daughter. I needed to ask myself about the potential

that my daughter could have in the future, serving Christ. The attitude of the prayer warrior is not just to inflict damage in the enemy camp, but to have a broader vision of what the battle is about. Hebrews 11:1 tells us that, *"Now faith is the substance of things hoped for, the evidence of things not seen."* When we pray for something we often focus on the problem, and the hopelessness which appears evident. An addiction to methamphetamines is a very real problem but, unless we believe that God is bigger than the problem, our prayers are weak.

4. While I was binding Satan in those areas I considered were controlling my daughter, I would do it at least once a day, and often at least three or four times a day. I prayed in other ways too. I prayed in her room, on her bed, out loud, and declared the word over her. I even lay on her floor, prostrate before God, asking Him to please bring her home. You may think this is over the top, and unnecessary, but in Deuteronomy 9:25, Moses pleads for God to spare the children of Israel, *"Thus I prostrated myself before the Lord; forty days and forty nights I kept prostrating myself, because the Lord had said He would destroy you."* Moses was determined God would not destroy his inheritance, and pleaded to God for their lives. So why shouldn't I do the same for my daughter?

I am reminded, in 1 Thessalonians 4:17 which is a very short verse, that it simply says, *"pray without ceasing."* God is always ready to hear our prayers, morning, noon, and night. He doesn't slumber or sleep. Last thing at night, first thing in the morning, whenever you need someone to speak to, He is there. My favourite place for prayer is in the car when I am alone. I can speak out loud, and use the time going to work, the grocery store, or visiting relatives, to speak to God about what is on my heart. I hear people say they have very little time for prayer, but it should become like breathing. If I am walking, I often ask God to remind me who to pray for. The Holy Spirit will bring someone, or something, into your mind.

The Scriptures also remind us that, to reach the Father, we need to pray to the Son. Jesus is our go between and, without Him, our prayers are going nowhere. 1 Timothy 2:5 tells us, *"For there is one God and one mediator between God and men, the man Christ Jesus."*

Imagine you are in the throne room of God, and you are kneeling at the feet of Jesus pouring out your heartfelt prayers. He then approaches the throne of His Father, and the Father asks: "What are the petitions today?"

Jesus replies, "I have a mother who is concerned about her daughter who is on drugs. This young woman lost her father as a young girl, and has struggled ever since. Father, she has given her testimony about my laying down My life for her, and was even baptised as a witness to her faith. Major disappointment has come into her life, and she has been enticed away by the wicked one. I am here to ask that We may intervene in this situation, and to ask if angels can be sent to protect her while We fight to bring her home."

I find it helps to use the imagination God gives us to envisage those things which we cannot see in the natural.

5. God loves persistence in prayer. I love this parable that Jesus taught from Luke 18:1-8. *"Then He spoke a parable to them, that men always ought to pray and not lose heart, saying: "There was in*

a certain city a judge who did not fear God nor regard man. Now there was a widow in that city; and she came to him, saying, 'Get justice for me from my adversary.' And he would not for a while; but afterward he said within himself, 'Though I do not fear God, nor regard man, yet because this widow troubles me I will avenge her, lest by her continual coming she weary me.'" Then the Lord said, "Hear what the unjust judge said. And shall God not avenge His own elect who cry out day and night to Him, though He bears long with them? I tell you that He will avenge them speedily..."

The message I get from this parable is to be persistent. We give up so easily when we pray. God is interested in our hearts toward Him. He wants us to keep on asking, and not to give up. Giving up at the beginning, or in the middle, of the battle is not an option. Persistence, consistency and, above all, faith is required when we pray. At the end of verse 8 of 1 Thess. Jesus says something which, at first, appears out of context. He says, *"...nevertheless, when the Son of Man comes will He really find faith on the Earth?"* I believe Jesus equates persistence with faith. To be persistent means to not give up. Faith doesn't give up, and neither would I.

6. Praying in the Spirit or in Tongues is something I would do at night. There were times my own words seemed inadequate. It is difficult when your loved one is away from home, and you don't know what is happening. At these times it is important to trust God, for He knows and He sees what we can't. The Bible says in Romans 8:26, *"Likewise the Spirit also helps in our weaknesses. For we do not know what we should pray for as we ought, but the Spirit*

Himself makes intercession for us with groanings which cannot be uttered."

I do not know what I am speaking when using Tongues, but God knows. 1 Corin. 14:2 says that, *"For he who speaks in a Tongue does not speak to men but to God, for no one understands him; however, in the Spirit he speaks mysteries."* Paul then concludes in 1 Corin. 14:15, *"What is the conclusion then? I will pray with the Spirit, and I will also pray with understanding..."* By praying in an unknown Tongue, it is the Spirit that makes intercession for us, but it is also important to pray with our understanding.

There was an interesting experiment carried out which used an MRI scanner to monitor the brain during times of prayer and meditation. It was found that during meditation or praying out loud, the frontal cortex of the brain is activated, and this was lit up on the MRI scanner. When a Christian speaks in an unknown Tongue, there is no frontal lobe activity apparent. I find that interesting, so it is not us who are praying but the Spirit in us!

Chapter 24

WEAPONS OF OUR WARFARE—THE WORD OF GOD

How do we overcome the negative aspect of what we see with our earthly eyes? This brings us to our next weapon of war. The Word of God.

Often in a crisis we become despondent, and this is because we are human. It is often the case that despondency leads us to become self-absorbed, and focus on our problems instead of on God and His solutions. It is so easy to stop reading the word, or cease to have our quiet time. It actually makes our time with God all the more important, especially the reading and meditation on God's word. I have found that the assaults and lies of the Devil increase when we are going through trauma or despair. The only way to combat Satan's lies is to meditate on the word, day and night. Commit it to memory.

I found it helpful to memorise certain verses which were specifically for my daughter. Sarah had asked Christ into her heart, and had given her testimony. I believed she now belonged to God, and He was not going to allow her to perish. I had two verses which I incorporated into my prayer for her, and would declare out loud. One of these was Philippians 1:6 which says, *"...being confident of this very thing, that he who has begun a good work in you (Sarah) will complete it until the day of Jesus Christ."* As I prayed, God, who had begun a good work in my daughter, was continuing to do that work until its completion. I was declaring to the Devil that my God was at work, whether I could see it in the flesh or not!

The other popular verse is in Jeremiah 29:11-13, *"For I know the thoughts I have towards you (Sarah), says the Lord, thoughts of peace and not of evil, to give you a future and a hope. Then you will call upon Me and go and pray to Me, and I will answer you. And you will seek Me and find Me, when you search for Me with your whole heart."*

Many people only use the beginning of these verses, about having a future and a hope, but my prayer was that my daughter would call upon the Lord herself, and search for Him with her whole heart. This would not happen for at least a year, but it did happen!

To continue in prayer and supplication, I also needed to build my own faith. In Romans 10:17, the Bible says: *"So then faith comes by hearing, and hearing by the word of God."* I read the word most often to myself but, when battling the enemy, I gain more faith by speaking it out loud. I like the thought that the enemy can hear me declare the truths in God's word. Jesus used the word to disarm the temptations of the Devil. It is possible He only spoke the word in His mind, but somehow I feel He would have spoken out loud, and with authority! Jesus used the written word of God to let the Devil know he had no power over Him. This is exactly the way we need to use the word of God – as a sword. It does damage to the enemy when we speak it out. I can see the principalities and powers cringing when we speak the word of God. Satan tried to give Jesus all the kingdoms of the world, if Jesus would worship him.

Jesus replied in Matthew 4:10, *"Get behind me, Satan! For it is written, 'You shall worship the Lord your God, and Him only you will serve.'"*

When depression and despair threatened to overcome me, it was easy to want to give up, but then I would remember, *"Through God we will do valiantly, for it is He who shall tread down our enemies."* (Psalm 60: 12)

My favourite verse is, *"I can do all things through Christ who strengthens me."* (Phil. 4:13)

Chapter 25

THE WEAPONS OF OUR WARFARE—PRAISE

The next weapon is praise and worship. This kept me going so many times when I was in danger of sinking into despair. When feeling despondent it is tempting to stop going to church, because you feel abandoned and unworthy, but of course this is not true because God would never abandon us. In fact, it is we who abandon Him. In times of trouble we need to press in to God. Continually remain in His presence.

Psalm 50:15 says, *"Call upon Me in the day of trouble; I will deliver you and you shall glorify Me."*

This is a promise that, when we call upon Him, He is with us. I kept going to church and worshipping my God and Saviour. Praise is a huge weapon against the enemy. Satan hates it when God is praised. Whether we are sad or glad we should praise Him and, by praising Him, we too are lifted up in spirit.

"Therefore by Him {Jesus} let us continually offer the sacrifice of praise to God, that is, the fruit of our lips, giving thanks to His name." (Hebrews 13:15)

Another favourite verse is found in Isaiah 61:3, *"To console those who mourn in Zion, to give them beauty for ashes, the oil of joy for mourning, the garment of praise for the spirit of heaviness."* In those moments of worship my mourning becomes joy.

At home I would put on my favourite praise and worship music, and sing and dance to the Lord. To lift up my voice and proclaim that He is Holy, and there is none like Him! I think of David and Miriam, who danced before the Lord with joy, without caring what anyone else thought. I lately had a prophesy said over me that 'Jesus loved to dance with me'. What a lovely picture of Jesus taking my hand in a Holy, joyful dance.

When I wasn't praying, I would play my praise and worship music in the car. At bedtime, when Satan would try to instil worry into my mind, to cause me sleeplessness, I would put on my worship CD and fall asleep praising Him. I would often fall asleep to one of my favourite songs; 'God will make a way' by Don Moen.

From Isaiah 43:19, *"…behold I do a new thing, now it shall spring forth: shall you not know it? I will even make a road in the wilderness, and rivers in the desert."*

If He can make rivers in the desert, then He can bring my daughter home!

Chapter 26

WEAPONS OF OUR WARFARE - FELLOWSHIP

God doesn't expect us to battle alone. We are made for relationship and, as Christians, we need each other as the Body of Christ. I have already mentioned the importance of continuing to attend church, and not forsaking meeting together.

Hebrews 10:24-25 says, *"And let us consider one another in order to stir up love and good works, not forsaking the assembling together, as is the manner of some, but exhorting one another, and so much the more as you see the day approaching."*

You have heard the saying, 'together we stand, divided we fall'. It is so important to have a united front when facing down the enemy. Psalm 133:1-2 tells us how special the bond of unity is among the brethren, *"Behold, how good and how pleasant it is for brethren to dwell in unity! It is like the precious oil upon the head..."*

There is also the passage that reminds us, *"Two are better than one, because they have a good reward for their labour. For if they fall, one will lift up his companion..."* (Eccle. 4:9-10)

There were many times of difficulty when a friend lifted me up, and I thank all those who were there for me.

The Bible also tells us, *"For where two or three are gathered together in My name, I am there in the midst of them."* (Matt. 18:20) God promises He is with you, and praying with others is powerful. Matt. 18:19 says, *"Again I say to you, if two of you agree on Earth concerning anything that they ask, it will be done for them by My Father in Heaven."*

At the time Sarah was in Bundaberg, I also practised spiritual warfare by joining a prayer group that prayed for the Nation of Australia. There were many topics we covered in those prayer sessions, and often the group would pray for Sarah. This was a great encouragement. When I was concerned about something happening in Bundaberg where Sarah was, the prayer leader, Michael, who had a gift of seeing in the Spirit, would see Sarah with God's hand upon her, which would help strengthen my faith.

These prayer meetings could be heavy going, because often Michael, and another man called Peter, would minister to people coming out of witchcraft. This is extremely difficult to give up because of the spiritual battle that follows. It was important to put on God's armour, and be covered in the blood of Christ when taking part in this type of prayer. Many would drop out of the group because of sickness, or onslaughts of depression. Before going to the prayer meeting, I would either get headaches or severe fatigue. I would have to fight through the desire to not go to the meeting. Once there, the fatigue or headaches would leave. I did have some attacks around the time I was involved in the group. It became part of my prayer life to put the armour on from Ephesians 6, and negate any curses coming against me. Christians don't realise that witches and Satanists pray against us. Of course they are not praying to Jesus, but to Satan!

One day, driving along the motorway, a four-wheel drive was in front of me towing a boat. Suddenly one of the rear wheels came off the trailer, and bounced towards my windscreen. Suddenly, it inexplicably did a 45-degree turn, and rolled across the centre island, straight across the two lanes on the other side of the motorway. It did not hit any vehicle! I believe this was a miracle, and I don't know whether an angel re-directed the tyre or not, but I believe that it had been headed for my car's windscreen, and it could well have been fatal if it hit me.

My own church played a huge part in keeping me focused and helping me not to give up on my daughter. I continued to be active in my church in helping lead worship, and was on the planning council. I would attend prayer meetings, and the church would pray for my daughter.

I also had a good friend who met with me frequently for prayer, and we attended the warfare group together. My friend, Heather, was from the Baptist church, and she hosted a Bible study group at her home where they would pray for Sarah. My pastor and his wife, who retired back to their farm in Gympie, also prayed for her. It was good to include anyone who knew Sarah, and to keep her covered in prayer by as many saints as possible. I like to imagine Jesus coming before the Father and, in His hand is a petition. Written on it are all the prayers that people have spoken for Sarah, which are presented before God.

There are many faithful Christians in the church who are struggling with family or friends who need prayer, but don't want anyone knowing what is going on. It is important to not let the enemy make us feel ashamed but, by having people pray, we are defeating the enemy. It may be that a small home group is a better place for sharing and praying, rather than the whole church. For us to be healed of our sin, we need to bring it to the light so God's Grace can restore us, or the one we love. It also means we are more effective in helping other people deal with their problems, and to know they are not alone.

Chapter 27

BACK TO BUNDABERG AGAIN

Since speaking to Drug Arm about my daughter and her drug addiction, I had been debating in my mind whether or not to take away the car. It was the means for her and Tim to get their drugs, and lead the lifestyle they were living. As a mother, I thought it would be putting my daughter in danger, and would make her more vulnerable without transport. God then reminded me that real love is love that disciplines. God treats us the same way.

In Hebrews 12:5-6 we are reminded, *"My son, do not despise the chastening of the Lord, nor be discouraged when you are rebuked by Him; for whom the Lord loves, He chastens, and scourges every son whom He receives."* If I believed this, then it was on me to do the right thing, and that was to take the car away from my daughter. It was registered in my name, and I was still paying for it. I also had to totally trust Sarah to God's protection.

I once more enlisted the help of my son, Aaron, with the intention of one of us driving Sarah's car and the other driving my car home.

I phoned Sarah and said, "Sarah, this is your mum. I feel that it's important that I take the car away as it's your way of getting the drugs that are causing you harm. Aaron and I will be up there on Saturday, and would like you to meet us at the shopping centre again."

"Mum, I understand you wanting the car, but it's our only means of getting around!"

"I realise that, Sarah. But it's registered in my name too, and I can't allow you both to do drug deals in a car I'm paying for!"

Sarah arranged for us to meet her at the same place at the shops and, on the Saturday, Aaron and I drove to Bundaberg which is a four-hour drive! We waited patiently for my daughter and Tim to show up, which seemed like ages. I honestly thought they may not show, and our whole trip would be for nothing! Finally my daughter appeared without Tim, looking very down and extremely thin. I tried not to look worried, but my instincts said to grab her and head back to Beerwah. But she is an adult child, so of course this was not going to happen. I made myself smile, and gave my daughter a big hug.

"How are you doing Sarah?" I asked.

Looking at the floor again, my daughter mumbled that she was fine. I got us some lunch, which Sarah picked at nervously, and I asked, "Is the car outside, Sarah?"

It was then she told me. "Tim took it to his mum and step dad's, even though I told him not to."

"Well, we will just have to go and get it then. You can come with us and show us where to go."

Sarah replied, "I need to go to the ladies' toilet, Mum, before we go."

Sarah left Aaron and I alone for what seemed like ages. At the time I thought nothing of it but, in hindsight, she was probably warning Tim that we were coming!

I drove Aaron and Sarah to Tim's mother's house, and his step-father met us outside. The car was sitting in the yard, so I assumed I would get the keys and drive it home.

I walked over to have a look at the vehicle, and was shocked that it was in such a state. It had only been about nine months ago that I had purchased the car for Sarah.

"Where is Tim?" I asked his step-father.

"He took off with a friend, like ten minutes ago. He seemed in a hurry."

Aaron went over and saw that the keys were in the car, and got in to try to start it. However, there was no response. He tried again. Nothing! Aaron popped the bonnet and went to look under the hood. Low and behold, the battery was missing!

Tim was obviously desperate to keep the car in Bundaberg, and had taken the battery out of the car so it couldn't be driven. Sarah and his step-father had no idea where he was, and I didn't have time to wait around, as we had a four-hour drive to get back home.

"I should have known he was up to something when he rang his friend to come and get him. He's hopeless, and good for nothing!" said Tim's step-father.

Although Tim's mother and step-father were concerned about my daughter, and very disparaging about Tim, there was nothing they could do to get him to come home. As frustrated as I was, I couldn't do anything but leave Sarah there with Tim's parents, and drive back to Beerwah, still unable to convince my daughter that she should come home. I could see the fight I had ahead of me, because Tim was a big part of the controlling force I was up against. He was determined to keep Sarah in Bundaberg at all costs.

The next time I went to Bundaberg was to pick up Sarah, and bring her home to meet her ex-boyfriend Lewis at the airport when he returned from Brazil. I know now it was not a good idea, but I desperately wanted my daughter back home, and off the drugs. I thought seeing Lewis might trigger some regret, and help her to re-think her life choices. It would take the long drive to Bundaberg to pick up Sarah, and another four hours back to Brisbane airport. I don't know how we got there on time, but we were there to meet him. All his family were there, and I regretted even more we went. Sarah looked so pale and thin, looking nervous and definitely not the beautiful, vibrant young woman she was when Lewis left a year ago.

In contrast, when Lewis got off the plane, here was this tall, suntanned young man who had let his hair grow, and looked so healthy and happy. The contrast between Lewis and Sarah was very marked, and I felt despair overwhelm me. Lewis hugged everyone, especially his parents and brother, and then aunts and uncles. He saw me, and I got a lovely hug too. Then he saw Sarah, whom he probably wasn't expecting, but gave her a quick hug. I don't know what would have gone through his mind, whether despair or maybe hope that they would rekindle what they had?

I knew it had been a long day, and we said goodbye to everyone as I drove Sarah home, still praying that it might have made a difference seeing her ex-boyfriend, whom she had been so happy with. As soon as we got back to the house, Sarah went to bed and slept soundly. A while later there was a knock at the door and, to my surprise, it was Lewis!

"Hi, Mrs Brown. I wondered if I could speak to Sarah for a few minutes?"

"I'm sorry, Lewis," I replied. "But Sarah is in bed asleep. It's been a long day for all of us."

He looked disappointed, but just said, "I brought her a gift back from Brazil which I wanted her to have."

"Thank you, Lewis. That was thoughtful of you," I replied.

The present he had for her was a lovely dress he had bought in Sao Paulo. I didn't know what to say, and I think he could feel my despair.

How do you explain to someone that the girl he loves is with a drug addict, and prefers that lifestyle to being with him. Of course it is not that easy to explain. Drug addiction is very real, and the brain and body need that next fix. It doesn't make sense, but you just look at people living on the street, often the result of alcohol and drug abuse. The power of addiction cannot be minimised.

"You look so well, Lewis, and it's good you're home, I'm sorry for everything that's happened. I'm sure it's been a shock for you, as it has for me. Would it be okay if we prayed before you go?"

So, before Lewis left, we prayed together for Sarah, and that was special. Perhaps that prayer kept alive the hope I had for my daughter, and this young man I had become fond of.

The next morning I hoped Sarah would stay awhile, but the pull of drugs, and Tim, had not dissipated miraculously overnight. She arranged for a friend to drive her back to Bundaberg. I remember when the friend arrived, saying to Sarah, "Please don't go!"

When I looked in her eyes as she pulled away from me, all I could see in her was someone else, and that someone else I did not like. I said to the Lord in my heart, "This is not my daughter, please bring her back to me!"

Chapter 28

MY OTHER CHILDREN BEAR MY LOAD

Despite what was happening to my daughter, I had to keep on living and look after my family. The ones left at home still needed me. I had two sons, Joe and Ben, my twins, who were in high school. I had to remind myself that these young men had no father, and I was all they had. Sarah had a younger sister, Leah, who was only 19 months younger than Sarah, but was so different in temperament. Leah was finishing her high school education, and would be graduating at the end of the year. Leah had no ambition to go to university and, two years before, along with her sister, Sarah, had been baptised at Ewan Maddock dam.

Despite everything that was going on with Sarah, my other three survived, and we managed from day to day. I can't say I was the perfect mother at this time. I know that my pre-occupation with the one who went astray, must have caused the other three to feel I wasn't always thinking about them, as I should. All three survived the dreadful pre-occupation I had, which reminded me of the parable that Jesus told of the shepherd who had 100 sheep. The shepherd was taking them back into the sheepfold, when he realised that one was missing. He could have said, "Well I need to look after the 99 sheep, and I just hope that the lost one will be alright". But he didn't. The shepherd went out of his way to find the one lost sheep, and did not sleep until it was returned to the fold with the other 99.

The prodigal son is another biblical story that I can relate to. We are all aware of the annoyance of the older son when the prodigal returned, and saw how this young man was again welcomed into the family. Was that all it was, or had this young man heard his father constantly lament over the loss of the younger sibling so much that he felt abandoned, and unseen? Why was this young man so angry at all the fuss that was made about his brother?

If I was the father or mother of the young man who left home, knowing that chances were that he would get into trouble, I would be praying and asking if he was alright. "I wonder where he is now," I would ask. "Could he be in prison?" Remember there was no social media or Facebook to check on, and you couldn't ring him up on the telephone to see how he was going! News would have come from someone passing, who had walked for miles on dusty roads.

I can understand this older brother's consternation at the fuss that was made! Did his father show his appreciation to the son who stayed home to help with the chores, and who may have dreams of his own he wanted to pursue?

I marvel at my three younger children surviving those days, and not just surviving but often thriving! Leah was to go on and do two years of Bible college, followed by two years of youth ministry teaching with Scripture Union. She quietly and sincerely followed her heart to be in ministry, despite the distraction of her mother at home for many of those years. I thank God that He is faithful, and does not cease working in each of us, no matter where we are in our walk with Him.

MY OTHER CHILDREN BEAR MY LOAD

It is a lesson that reminds us that we need to love and appreciate those of our children who stay close, who do the right thing, and are there for us when we are distracted. As parents we are still responsible for their security, and love, even when we are feeling overwhelmed. Thankfully, there were others outside the family, and older siblings, who could step in and support my children when I could not.

I also believe that the way we, as parents, deal with stressful situations helps our children to also deal with stress in a positive way. I spent a lot of time in prayer. I continued to go to church, and spent time with others in prayer. When feeling down and hopeless, I would put on my praise and worship music to lift me up. I would try to make time for my other children's extra activities, like football and athletics. I was not a perfect mother, and stress would have been evident many times, but holding onto my God, and my faith, I believe would give my children an idea of what living the Christian life of faith was all about. Many times in the years ahead, my children would speak faith words into my life, and get me through difficult situations!

Chapter 29

GOD KEEPS HER SAFE

It is difficult being a parent, even when things are going well. To live the Christian life as an example for our children, and to teach them the ways of God, are so important. When, despite our best intentions, things go wrong, it can be extremely discouraging. This is when we need to remind ourselves that the Devil looks at each of our children as potential threats to his kingdom. As Christians, we need not be surprised by what will come against them. I recognised the potential my daughter had to inflict damage in the enemy camp.

On one occasion, when Sarah came home briefly, I sat with her and told her, "You are a child of God, and He will not let you go! Whatever you, and your boyfriend, get up to, expect it not to be easy. The Lord will not let you go without a fight." It may sound like I was invoking God's wrath, and putting my child in harm's way. I expected her life to be difficult, but protected. There were many examples of this.

I was at a Bible study with my friend, Heather, and a group of ladies, and as we were having coffee I received a phone call from an unusual source.

"Hello, this is Roberta. How can I help you?"

"Hello, Mrs Brown. This is RACQ roadside assist, and we are in Bundaberg. We have had a call from you daughter, Sarah, who says she is broken down and has no money to pay for membership. Sarah asked if we could ring you, and see if you would be willing to pay her membership. Because she is only eighteen, it's thirty dollars for the year. Would you be able to do that, Mrs Brown?"

"Where is she? Is she alright?"

"Mrs Brown, she is between Bundaberg and Childers somewhere. Our roadside assist team will do everything to find her. Are you willing to pay for membership?"

I had every right to refuse, as they were spending all their money on drugs, alcohol, and cigarettes, but I needed to keep her safe, and who knew where she was. It's a long way between Childers and Bundaberg!

"Yes, of course I'll pay for her. But please find her!"

They took my debit card details, and they told me they would do everything to find her and not to worry. I paid the money, prayed she would be alright, and that they would be able to help her. What happened next would test my faith once again, as myself, and the ladies present, would pray even more.

After about ten minutes, the phone rang again. "Hello. Roberta here."

"Hello, Mrs Brown. It's roadside assist again. We needed to let you know that we have lost contact with your daughter, and cannot get her on the phone."

My daughter was somewhere along a large stretch of road, in the heat, unable to start her car, and no one knew where she was! Many of you reading this will not be from Australia, so you may not appreciate the long stretches of road here, where there is nothing for miles. I assumed that Sarah was on the main Childers to Bundaberg road, so she would be easy to spot in her dilapidated Nissan.

This is where I commend the RACQ, roadside assist, who realised that they not only had a lost young woman on her own, broken down somewhere, but also a very worried mother on the Sunshine Coast, four hours away unable to do anything but pray! Often this is where God wants us to be, utterly dependent on him!

"Mrs Brown, we know this is very worrying for you, but I can assure you that we will do everything we can to locate and help your daughter. We intend to send a tow truck half way to Childers from Bundaberg, and a tow truck half way from Bundaberg to Childers, to cover the whole area until we locate her."

This was way beyond what I would have expected. They also assured me they would ring me back once they had located Sarah and the car. I was so grateful that I had women of faith with me, and those amazing people who worked for RACQ! All I could do was pray, and wait.

I had yet another call from them to say that, although they had driven from Bundaberg to Childers, they had not found the car! This was even more disturbing. Where was she?

I would not hear any more for another four hours! This is when our faith is tested. I left my friends and was shopping that afternoon, and had to continually let God know that I trusted Him with my daughter. No matter where our children are in this world, we need to trust them to the Lord. To pray, and then continue to worry, is not faith. We have to fully believe that He is in control, and that His angels are with them.

There are examples of faith found everywhere in Scripture. Hebrews chapter 11 is the great faith chapter, which many know so well. I love the passage found in Matthew 8:5-10 about the Centurion who had a servant who was paralysed. First of all, he came to Jesus because he believed He could heal his servant. Jesus tells him He will come to the servant, but hear what the Centurion says next. In verse 8 it says, *"Lord, I am not worthy* that You should come under my roof. But only speak a word, and my servant will be healed." What faith is that! If only we had that sort of faith in the church today! He recognised the authority that Jesus had, and the power to accomplish the healing of his servant. Jesus replies in verse 10, *"I say to you, I have not found such great faith, not even in Israel!"*

To grow our faith we need to practise it. I believe the more we trust God, the more He will do. Even if you struggle to believe speak out the words: "I believe Lord!" Our words have power, even when our hearts are faint. I had to continually remind myself that God was in control of the situation, and that Sarah would be safe.

Late in the afternoon I received a call. "Mrs Brown, this is the RACQ and we have good news. We have had a phone call from your daughter to tell us that she managed to get the car started, and is safe!"

"Thank you so much. I appreciate all you have done, and I'm so glad to hear this news."

My daughter had been able to get her car started and, when she had a signal, rang the RACQ to let them know she was alright. How was her car able to start? Was this an answer to our prayers? Psalm 91:11 says: *"For He shall give his angels charge over you, to keep you in all your ways."* I often ask God to send his angels to protect my children and grandchildren. The RACQ sent out those tow trucks, and did not see my daughter's car. Why did they not see it? It was because it was not broken down on the main road, but on a very quiet, countryside road. All I can say is that He is faithful!

The Lord protected Sarah in many more instances. One night, at the place they were staying, her boyfriend fell asleep with a lit cigarette and nearly set the house on fire. Another time Sarah collapsed after a very bad drug experience. This scared my daughter, and she rang me. My friend, Heather, just happened to be in Bundaberg at the time, and was able to pick her up and bring her home. There were many dangerous situations that Sarah found herself in. Her boyfriend would often leave her somewhere alone, while he took off in the car to look for drugs. They also owed drug dealers money, and were in danger of having their lives threatened. This is how eventually God really got my daughter's attention!

Chapter 30

I DECIDE TO FINALLY TAKE THE CAR AWAY!

God finally convinced me yet again to take away the physical means by which my daughter was getting around, with her boyfriend to obtain their drugs. I was to go to Bundaberg and bring the car home! Again, I asked my eldest son, Aaron, to accompany me to Bundaberg in my car, and Aaron would drive my car back while I drove Sarah's.

Some might wonder if I had the right to take the car from my daughter. The car was registered to me, and Sarah, and I had borrowed money to pay for the car with the understanding that Sarah would pay me back when she had a job. The reason I bought the car was for her safety while attending dance classes where there was very poor public transport. I never dreamed she would take off to Bundaberg in it, and it would become a means to get their next drug fix!

I believe that God loves each of us, and knows what we need even more than we do. The Bible says that He chastises those He loves. In Proverbs 3:11-12 it reminds us, *"My son (daughter) do not despise the Lord's discipline, and do not resent His rebuke, because the Lord disciplines those He loves, as a father the son he delights in."* It is difficult to delight in disobedience, especially when that disobedience can cause permanent harm and even death! This is what is known as tough love, and is not always easy to do because we want blessings for our children, and their prosperity. Here's the crunch, by loving them in an ungodly way we actually deny them God's blessings in the future. We may also deny God the blessing that our children could become to Him!

The morning came when I was going to go and get the car. I prayed that Sarah would be at the shopping centre to meet us, like she said she would. As usual, Aaron and I waited patiently, and inwardly I prayed.

In this she was obedient and, although Aaron and I had to wait a while for her to meet us, she did come. It was always difficult to look at my beautiful daughter, and to see her thin and pale, a shadow of what she was like. She had always been slim and athletic, but now she was painfully thin, and her hair was dull and lifeless. There were marks on her arms where she had scratched herself, and there was little care for her appearance.

Young people, don't let yourselves be encouraged to think that pills or needles can solve your problems. Life is not easy, but God provided Jesus who already suffered and died for you! John 10:10 says, *"The Thief does not come but to steal, kill and destroy. I have come that they may have life, and that they may have it abundantly."* Jesus will give you an abundant life, but the enemy will give you death and destruction.

"Sarah, it's good to see you!" I said as she arrived, minus Tim again.

"Fine, Mum," she replied. "It's good to see you too!"

Sarah seemed not at all nervous, and genuinely did seem to be glad to see me. I wondered what was going on, and why she seemed so compliant. I was yet to see the car!

At the time we came to take the car, Sarah and Tim were living with a single mother and her four children. She was on welfare, and was also

I DECIDE TO FINALLY TAKE THE CAR AWAY!

an alcoholic. So two drug addicts, an alcoholic, and four children in the middle. I am not judging this mother, and I am sure she loved her children. It was just a sad state of affairs, and one which is compounded many times around the world! It was not unusual for me to get a message, on my phone while at work, from Sarah to say they had no money for food, and would I send a few dollars so they could buy bread and milk for the children. They knew what buttons to push. I was concerned for the children too, and would send fifty dollars now and then, with great trepidation.

Sarah, Aaron, and I went to see the car where Sarah had parked it. It looked nothing like the car I had bought for her. It was in quite a state, and I was wondering how I was going to get it back to the Sunshine Coast without breaking down! The bonnet was tied down with wire, and the front grill of the car was missing! The smell inside was not pleasant either. To add to this, my daughter informed me that there was no first gear, and it would need to be started in second. The other factor was that the Bundaberg police knew the car, and often followed Sarah and Tim around hoping to catch themselves a major drug dealer! So here I was, going to attempt to drive this car four hours down a highway to Beerwah, with no first gear, and I wondered if the police would stop me before I got half way home. It was clearly an unroadworthy vehicle! Sarah drove us to the house where she was staying, and she got out of the car, and I got in the driver's seat. Now it did occur to me to just leave the bomb of a car there, but I realised they were counting on me not taking the car because of the state it was in.

"Lord," I prayed, as I sat in the dilapidated version of what used to be a decent car. "Please give me courage and strength to drive this car home to Beerwah, and get me home safely! I pray my beautiful daughter will decide to come home with me, when she realises I am serious about taking the vehicle away!"

I knew that if anything happened, Aaron would be driving behind me all the way in my car.

I was sitting in the car with the window down ready to leave, and I looked at my daughter and I said, "Sarah please come home, this is not the place for you." She shook her head at me and refused to go. I fought to hold back the tears, as I said goodbye, not knowing when I would ever see her again. I started the car up, and began to chug down the road in second gear, broken-hearted at having to leave my beloved daughter behind once again!

Leaving Bundaberg was a challenge. I dreaded every red light, which meant I would have to stop the car, and then hear the gears grinding as I started it up again in second. I also prayed there would be no hills! My first test came as I was filling the car with petrol. I noticed a police car, parked in the car park of the petrol station. I tried to keep calm, and signalled to Aaron I was ready to go, self-consciously chugging out of the driveway onto the main road. I breathed a sigh of relief when I realised the police car remained where it was, only to pass another one on my way out of town! If I was driving anywhere else other than Bundaberg, I would have been pulled off the road for a check, but no one stopped me. Another police car passed me on the road, and never stopped me. I do believe God was with me, and somehow blinded them to the state of the car!

It was a straight run until, after three hours, I decided I needed a rest. My nerves were shattered driving a car I was concerned would break down any minute! We stopped at a major service centre for something to eat and the restroom. Feeling more confident that we would be home in another hour, I got in the car and, in front of many onlookers, started the car up in second. It was not a pretty sight, with the tied down bonnet and missing front end! I was able to back out in reverse, but got stuck in second, with the car refusing to move forward. As people stared, I became more and more flustered. Saying a silent prayer, I turned off the car, and started it again, flooring the accelerator, and kangaroo hopping up the car park! I can laugh now, but it wasn't so funny then!

The next test was still getting home without being stopped by police! "Lord," I said. "Please get me home safely, and without being stopped!" I was approaching the off ramp to go around a curve and up onto the overpass, and knew if I had to stop for someone coming the other way it would be nearly impossible to get the car moving again. Once more I asked God to give me the all clear, and He did, and I kept driving in third on to the overpass. Nearly home. It was with great relief when Aaron and I arrived back at the house in Beerwah. I drove the car up an incline, and parked it so it wouldn't be in the way. I was glad to make it back in one piece, but saddened to have to leave Sarah behind again. I was exhausted, but not downtrodden. I resolved even more to keep fighting on my knees and, to be honest, I believe it was then I felt closer to victory!

Chapter 31

LIFE GOES ON, SO DOES THE FIGHT

Taking my daughter's only means of transport was not easy and, in the coming weeks, I would wonder if I had done the right thing. I needn't have worried, as Tim and my daughter were very resourceful. They found a bike somewhere, and would cycle to the shops and back. I received the odd message from Sarah, which was reassuring, but also troubling as she would invariably want money when their government payments would run out. I am not saying I did the right thing in giving them any money and, even though it was only 50 dollars at a time, it probably didn't help matters!

I had to keep working, and looking after my other children. I continued with my local church, and meeting with my spiritual warfare group on Monday nights. During this time, most of my waking moments were spent in prayer for Sarah. As I drove to work, I would pray and bind all spirits I believed were affecting my daughter. The spirits of anti-Christ, spirits of addiction, and one which seems to go with the addictive personality – the spirit of control. The addictive personality is one which wants to desperately control everything and, when they can't for any reason, they turn to addiction. It could be drugs, alcohol, gambling, or pornography.

Another major ruling spirit here is the spirit of rebellion and rejection. These go together, and are usually manifest in childhood. Something occurs in childhood which allows this spirit to become dominant in the person's life. This spirit is also connected to mental illness. In some it can produce symptoms of bipolar and schizophrenia.

In Tim, God showed me a young boy standing forlornly, looking at his feet in shame. According to my daughter, Tim had suffered as a child. His mother had him when she was only sixteen, and he never knew his father. The first time I met Tim was when Sarah turned 18, and I didn't know much about him, but I felt uncomfortable as he couldn't look me in the eye. This is a symptom of shame, and one which I would come to recognise when dealing with another young man who came into my life later. I had a bad feeling from the start about this relationship between my daughter and Tim.

Tim bore the spirit of rejection because he had no father, and felt abandoned. His step-father was not one to affirm him, so he never felt he could measure up to expectations. He felt destined to fail at whatever he did. Because of this, he invariably acted out that failure in rebellion. Examples of this were the fact that he was a trained plumber, and could easily make $1,000 per week if he wanted to. He had been working, and then something made him go off suddenly on a drug binge, and chuck in his job. I believe the cause was being constantly assaulted with negative self-talk. Every negative word spoken to him would come into his mind. Feelings of inadequacy and depression. Drugs became a way of blocking out these negative voices. God taught me a lot through Tim. He taught me to look behind the person's struggles, to the pain that lay beneath. I first saw a rebellious young man who was no good. God showed me a frightened, confused boy, who had never really grown up and, despite many good qualities, would be haunted by his past. As I got to know his circumstances better, I would understand him more and more.

At the beginning the only one I was concerned with was my daughter. I selfishly believed that Tim was the reason she was on drugs, and I prayed many times that God would take him out of the picture. He was a roadblock to getting my daughter back!

Meanwhile I kept praying, and part of that prayer would be binding those spirits of control, and then to loose into Sarah those that were the opposite. First for the Holy Spirit to influence her, and for her to sense God's presence. The spirit of repentance, love, joy, peace, and a desire for the things of God, once more. You might ask what proof there was that this worked, and all I can say is she came back with a growing resolve to get her old life back; or perhaps a new life in Christ was what she really needed. You can be a believer, but have no idea of the power of Grace in your life, and in the change the Holy Spirit can make! There are many Christians who go through the motions of being a Christian, but have not had the born-again experience. To really know the power of Grace, God's forgiveness, and the enormity of what was achieved by Christ on the cross! If anything, Sarah knows the power of that Grace better than anyone. Sarah would tell me later that, as she was lying in bed, she would feel God's presence at times, and I believe it was when I was binding those spirits of control, and loosing into her the power of the Holy Spirit! My daughter also told of times of spiritual attack, when something would try to suffocate her in the night and she felt an evil presence. Was this a struggle between God and Satan for my daughter's life? There is no doubt in my mind that it was.

Of course, Satan attacked me too at this time, mainly with doubt and fear. It was worse at night when I would try to sleep, and the thoughts would assail me. Where is she? Is she safe, or lying in a ditch somewhere?

I needed to replace the fear thoughts with the word of God! I would recall verses to counteract the fear, and verses that I would speak over Sarah. One which I have already mentioned was from Jeremiah 29:11, and also Philippians 1:6. I was declaring that God was doing something in Sarah's life, and she had a future which was not apparent with ordinary eyes, but was clear with spiritual eyes. When Satan tried to convince me that I would lose my daughter, I would declare that God had plans for her, and I would not accept the Devil's lies!

That verse from 2Timothy 1:7 was, *"For God has not given us a spirit of fear; but of power and of love and of a sound mind."*. Notice that fear is called a 'spirit of fear', not just fear!

I would pray before bed, and also play my praise and worship music on my CD player. No matter how despondent I would become, I would always end the day praising my God. Praising God is the best way to banish Satan's attacks. 'No weapon of war formed against me' and my daughter was going to prosper! From Isaiah 54:17 I was in the wilderness, but God's hand was leading me through.

Chapter 32

SHARING THE LOAD

In all our troubles there is one thing we must not do, and that is to battle on alone. There is a saying, 'that together we stand and divided we fall'. The enemy wants to divide and conquer. If he can separate the brethren, and cause dissension to keep us apart, then he will try to do just that. The mistake that Christians make is to hide their problems from one another. Often Satan will use shame, fear, and pride to stop us from getting the support we need when dealing with our difficulties. These difficulties take many forms. It can be a troubled teenager, someone with a disability in the family, even a relationship breakdown, such as marital issues and addictions.

Being a Christian seems to mean to most people that problems will never come their way. The usual stresses and relationship issues are not supposed to happen to us! Our children will be perfect because we have brought them up as loving, obedient, and church going. Nothing can go wrong as long as we take them to church, and read and pray with them at home. But things do go wrong, sickness does come, and relationships do break down. As Christians, what can we do when these things happen?

It is often very difficult for some to open up, and be honest about the difficulties they are facing. And Satan is counting on just that! Separate the brethren, confide in no-one, hide your true feelings and your struggles. Keep the dirty linen in the closet!

Now I am not saying that you should confide in everyone, or shout your problems to the rooftops. I recommend belonging to a home group, or finding an intercessor you can relate to, and share your confidences with.

I did speak to those I shouldn't have about my daughter. It was difficult not to, especially at work. There were those who were not Christians who had experiences of their own and, of course, they often had negative outcomes. I was told that if your child became involved with drugs that there was no hope, and I would probably not see my daughter again. I was told to look after myself, because there was nothing I could do to save my daughter, so accept it.

The danger with listening to this kind of well-meaning talk is that you begin to doubt that something can be done. Your faith takes a battering, and depression and self-pity can set in. This is not the way of the Christian. Our faith needs to be guarded or we are in danger of losing it. It needs nurturing, testing, and used on a daily basis for it to grow and become strong. We also need to surround ourselves with other people of faith, believers, prayer warriors, and intercessors. Intercession is a powerful tool and the greater your faith the more power your intercession. I needed intercessors of faith to stand with me in the battle, and to proclaim the truth of God's word. It was to those intercessors I would go.

The Lord also rewards persistence in prayer, and I never let up bringing my petitions to Him every day. It is also important to have a particular prayer partner. Someone who understands the situation and can stand with you, encourage you, and pray with you, especially at times of crisis. I would spend a lot of time with one particular Christian friend, my spiritual warfare group, an ex-pastor and his wife, and my own church group. If there was a visiting healing evangelist I would go forward for prayer on behalf of my daughter. Family members also stood in the gap to believe for Sarah.

While in the battle we need to be fed ourselves, and to fill our tank of faith. It is easy to become discouraged and anxious. I would make more effort to read my Bible, and to read books of faith and intercession by well-known prayer warriors. Books by Cindy Jacobs and Dutch Sheets, or by those who have testimonies to share. Our testimony is very important, and we all have one. One of the books that encouraged me was the book called 'Intercessory Prayer' by Dutch Sheets. It was what I needed to help me use as many weapons of warfare as possible. His personal testimonies of faith stand out.

There was one particular day that I decided to seek out a Christian friend, who was also the mother of a young man who had been a friend of Sarah's. She understood early on, even before the drugs, that my daughter wasn't doing so well. It was her son who had come across my daughter taking the pills, which led to her going to hospital mentioned at the beginning of this book. He had alerted the teacher to what Sarah was doing, which helped prevent side effects, such as liver failure. It also gave me the knowledge that there were problems in my daughter's life.

I rang my friend and we met for prayer. It was an intense time of intercession. The tears streamed down my face as I poured my heart out to God. At one point my friend had her hand on my back to comfort me. I remember clearly feeling the pressure of that hand on me all through the time of prayer, only to open my eyes and realise that my friend's hand was no longer there. I felt so strongly that it was God's presence, or an angel, that I felt with me. God understands our anguish for our loved ones, and is there to comfort us.

Chapter 33

THE CAR IS GONE AGAIN!

Somehow the car ends up back in Bundaberg with my daughter and Tim. I felt like it was too much to try to get it back after I had gone through so much to get it the first time. My God had other plans, and He was determined to use the car as part of the means to convince my daughter that the life she was leading was not going to end well.

I don't know how the car ended up back in Bundaberg. It is a foggy patch in my memory, and no doubt there was a bit of manipulation involved. There were many times that Sarah came home, and I would try to convince her to stay. Perhaps one of these times I had gone to work, or left her on her own, but however it happened, the car once again was used to get around for work and drugs. Sometimes Tim and Sarah would do fruit or vegetable picking, and once Sarah got a few hours a week in a hotel bar. But more often than not they would lose their jobs because of the drug habit. They were unreliable and often, when Sarah needed to get to work in Childers, Tim would take off in the car leaving her stranded.

One day, which happened to be the same day that I met the mother of Sarah's friend for prayer, Sarah had been out in the car in Bundaberg without Tim. That afternoon, after my time of prayer, I received a very distressed call from Sarah. She phoned to say she was stranded without the car. Sarah had been out without Tim, and bumped into a chap whom they owed money to for drugs. Not able to get the money they owed him, he decided to take Sarah's car keys and drove off with the car. He told her they wouldn't get it back until they paid what they owed. Now I should have been very upset at this occurrence but, in actual fact, I was very calm. I felt that this was God's doing, and He had taken the car away to show my daughter how futile her lifestyle was.

Many months before I had attended a Wesleyan church annual conference, and had met a pastor who was known to my pastor and his wife. He was from Bundaberg, and my pastors and myself shared about the problems I was having with my daughter. He said that any time I needed someone to help Sarah, or talk to her, I just had to call him. This was the time when I needed some help for Sarah. I gave her his phone number, and she was able to ring him to help her out.

"Hello my name is Sarah. My mum told me she met you at a conference on the Sunshine Coast. I am having a bit of trouble, and my mum said you might be able to help me."

"Sarah. Yes, I believe I met your mother at Coolum, with Pastor Lionel and Jan. What can I do to help you?"

"I was on my own without my boyfriend, and a drug dealer we owed money to took my car, and has left me stranded. I wondered if you could pick me up and give me a lift back to my place?"

The pastor replied, "I would be happy to help you out, Sarah. Where are you?"

Sarah told the pastor where she was, and he picked her up.

Sarah said, "I am really grateful for your help, pastor, as I had no money to get a taxi."

THE CAR IS GONE AGAIN!

"I am pleased to be able to help you, for your sake, but also for your mother's as she is very concerned for you and the lifestyle you are leading. I think the best fatherly advice I can give is to try to make it home, and get help for your drug addiction. God loves you, and this way of life is not for a beautiful young girl like yourself!"

After this fatherly talk he dropped her off, and told her if she needed anything to let him know. Remember, Sarah had no father to affirm her, and this simple input into my daughter's life would help in her decision to return home. Meanwhile, the car was still in the hands of the drug dealer. I didn't panic at what had happened, I was sure everything was working out for the good of God's plan.

I spoke calmly to Sarah on the phone, and told her that the car was registered to me too, and to tell the drug dealer that I would ring the police and report it stolen. Within an hour the car was brought back to Sarah. But it had an impact on the future, as it showed just how out of control her life was! My daughter spoke of coming home soon after this incident with the car, and I held onto the belief that God was at work, and I would soon have her back. But still my faith was tested.

Can I encourage you, if you are a Christian man or woman, to speak a positive word into the life of a young person, especially those who have struggled growing up, or who are from single-parent families. They need affirmation and loving guidance and, most of all, encouragement. Life can be tough, and hearing some words of wisdom, or letting them know how special they are, can make a big difference in a young person's life. It is easy to look down on troubled and wayward teenagers, and be judgemental. We don't know what they have been through, or what their home life is like. Let them know that God loves them, even if He doesn't like their behaviour.

Chapter 34

I LEARN AN IMPORTANT LESSON

I continued to pray for my daughter and, to my shame I also prayed that God would take away the person whom, I believed, was keeping her in Bundaberg and from returning home. I prayed that Sarah would tire of Tim, and leave him, but the ties that bound them together were strong. I asked the Lord what I should do, and He reminded me that Tim was lost too. Didn't he deserve God's Grace, just as much as Sarah? I was very resistant, but finally decided that, if it would bring my daughter back, then I would pray for him too. I began to pray fervently for both of these lost young people.

Meanwhile Lewis, Sarah's ex-boyfriend, asked if the twins, Leah, and myself, would like to go with him, his mother, and some friends to the football. It was a Rugby League game, which is very popular in Australia, and it was between two Queensland teams – the Brisbane Broncos and the Gold Coast Titans. We took the train down to Brisbane, and it was exciting. This was actually my very first live game, although I had seen many games on TV. The atmosphere in person was so different from watching

I LEARN AN IMPORTANT LESSON

at home, with flags waving and fans dressed in their team's colours. Lewis and his mum had their Broncos colours on, and we all waited for the game to begin as the stadium filled with fans from both sides. Suncorp Stadium is in the middle of Brisbane city, and is the home of the Brisbane Broncos. The Titans come from the Gold Coast, which is an hour from Brisbane.

The game started and, although I usually only watch the football when finals are on, it was different being at a live game. Both sides were playing well, and the crowds cheered on their teams as the minutes counted down. In the last ten minutes, the Titans scored and the Broncos fans became dejected, thinking that the game was all but over. In my mind, I started to liken it to the despondency I felt over Sarah still not coming home. In that, moment God challenged me about my faith, and that I needed to continue to believe in the mighty power and faithfulness of my God. So I silently spoke to Him, and said: "Well, if the Broncos can win this game, then I know my daughter is coming home, even when everything is stacked against us!"

In minutes just before the final horn sounded, one of the Broncos' star players ran down the middle of the field, and scored a field goal right between the goal posts. Amazing! But it was not over, as this just evened the score. Extra time was called, and play went on. The first team to score would win the match. It was nerve wracking stuff. Then, again, the Broncos kicked a field goal but, instead of the ball going through the goal, it hit the left-hand goal post. In those seconds, everyone thought the game was lost, but miracles do happen! The ball hit the inside of the goal post, and bounced at right-angles, hitting the right goal post. Somehow it bounced from there through both goal posts, scoring the winning goal, allowing the Broncos to claim victory! It was the craziest thing I had ever seen in football. Although those who were with me were unaware of my prayers, and the struggle of faith going on inside me, I realised I needed not fear, as God was definitely in control!

I continued to pray with fervour, and committed to praying at my spiritual warfare group. I sensed, in my spirit, that the time was drawing close for Sarah to return, and I needed to dig in. Many who intercede for something often give up, just before breakthrough. When we are at our weariest, we must press on! Around this time, there was a Christian visiting our area who had a prophetic gifting. He was giving many encouraging words to people, like my daughter, Leah, and her Christian friend, and I felt I needed some encouragement from the Lord too. Near the end of the meeting, I finally had him pray for me.

The only thing he could say was that witches were praying against me! If there was any doubt I was in a spiritual battle, it was dispelled. This man knew nothing of my background, or that I was in a fight for my daughter, or that I belonged to a spiritual warfare group. But he did see the enemy try to influence me, and come against me. God knows why it is worth fighting, and the Devil knows why he needs to interfere with our plans, but do we Christians know the importance of following the Lord's promptings to intercede?

Chapter 35

HOME AT LAST

Breakthrough was coming and, before long, I received a text message from Sarah to say she was coming home. I was overjoyed, as you can imagine, but then came the condition; that Tim would be coming too! I had prayed for him, and been obedient to God in this, but I wasn't fully prepared for this young man to come into my home.

My heart sank, as deep down I felt that, even if he became a Christian, he was so different from Sarah. I could imagine the frustration that would come from this relationship in the future. I know that God is a miracle working God, and can sustain even the most difficult relationship, but often relationships born in sin often become unstuck, as they soon discover that there is little in common. I had to see beyond the here and now, and trust God with the future. Walking in faith is a constant exercise of trusting God, for only He knows the way forward.

They arrived from Bundaberg in the battered Nissan Pulsar. They came in the door, and seemed very happy to be there. God only knows the conversation between them that led to the decision to get in the car, and to change the direction they were going. I am not naive enough to think that they had suddenly become righteous, and were ready to jump to God's command! No, on the contrary, I knew that there was a long road ahead. I was dealing with two methamphetamine addicts, and I had to stay on my toes and keep praying. I needed to keep believing and, most of all, love them with the love of Christ. I would be tested, again and again. I didn't pull any punches, though, as I told them of the importance of needing Christ. I knew that the decision to follow Christ would make the transition away from drugs much easier.

Something I will never forget was a remark that Tim made soon after arriving at my home. He said, "As soon as I walked in the door, I felt safe."

I believe what he felt was the presence of the Holy Spirit. Something that was foreign to him. I had to lay down rules, of course. There was to be no sleeping together, no drugs, no alcohol, and the only concession I made was that they would only be able to smoke outside.

At first they were more than eager to please me, as I was providing food, shelter, and a place away from drug dealers! Tim would go out of his way to impress me by making cups of tea, doing the dishes, and even helping with the shopping. I had the impression, once more, of a young boy in a man's body, trying desperately to earn approval.

The difficult part of all this was trusting them, as I was not ignorant to the up-and-down nature of drug addiction. I have dealt with drug addicts in my job as a nurse, and they are extremely manipulative and difficult to deal with. In a hospital situation they can also be very demanding of your time and energy. Here I was, a single mother having to deal with two of them in my own home!

The main thing was to try to get them both professional help, as I was not used to coping with addicts. I had been looking for help for Sarah for some time. One of the ministries I had come across, while Sarah was at school, was a group called 'Mercy Ministries'. They had a house on the

Sunshine Coast, were Christian, and dealt with issues in young women. Some of these were eating disorders, self-harming, drug and alcohol abuse, and depression. It sounded like the perfect solution for Sarah. They had a Bible based program which helped bring the girls a knowledge of Christ, His work on the cross, and how God loved them. It gave them the ability to replace the negative messages with positive ones, from the word of God.

At the time Sarah was at school, I was concerned about her being anorexic, and was able to speak to someone from Mercy Ministries. I was somewhat disappointed at the response, as they felt that, with limited spaces available, Sarah was not bad enough to need their help! At the time I didn't know where to turn, and felt let down. Part of me wondered that, if Sarah had gone there at that time, then maybe she would not have gone through drug addiction, and things may have been very different. A lot of the pain that both Sarah and I went through may have been circumvented, but God had to remind me that, *"...we know that all things work together for good to those who love God, to those who are called according to His purpose."* (Romans 8:28)

I believe that what we experience in life, both good and bad, are for God's purpose, and He will use our brokenness, and our victories, to reach others for Christ. But this contact with Mercy Ministries would not be wasted, and the Lord was yet to use them in my daughter's life. One day, when Sarah was home previously, I had opened the website on the computer and had shown her what they were about. The most frustrating thing about trying to help a loved one win the battle against drugs, is that they are of an age which prohibits us, as parents, getting help on their behalf. The decision to get help has to come from the person them self. They have to own the problem, and seek help for it.

I could show Sarah the website, and point her in the right direction, but the choice to get help was hers, and hers alone. Prayer was the key, and what I could not accomplish, the Holy Spirit could. One day, when Sarah was home, I discovered she had printed off all the application forms for Mercy Ministries and, although this was a small step forward in the natural world, it was a huge step forward in the spiritual battle of the mind.

Chapter 36

A MOVIE, A MAN OF GOD, AND AN EX-DRUG ADDICT

Once Tim and Sarah were under my roof, I felt a responsibility to share the Gospel with them so that Christ could work from the inside, and help them overcome the obstacles in the way of recovery from addiction. Church was alien to Tim, and it was difficult to get him to go. A healing evangelist, John Mellor, was at a church on the Coast. He had a Holy Spirit anointing to pray for the sick, and thousands have been healed through his ministry.

I felt that Sarah should have prayer and, although addictions are psychological, they are also physical, and I felt a touch from God was what my daughter badly needed. She had been a Christian, so was no stranger to going to church. I managed to drive them both to the church and, we were going in to sit down, when Tim suddenly began to get agitated and wouldn't stay. He wanted to go outside. I left him to it, and sat down with Sarah. John's meetings can be long because he makes it his mission, before he prays with people for healing, to preach the Gospel of Salvation first. This is because often non-Christians come to the meetings, and it gives the glory to Jesus when people are healed and released from pain. To John the importance of healing was secondary to the gospel being preached.

I had to keep praying for Sarah to go forward towards the end of the meeting and, eventually, she was able to go up, and John prayed for her. At that moment, Tim returned in time to see the anointing touch Sarah, and her fall on the floor! This, of course, made him react even more, and he again headed out the door, possibly worried he'd be on the floor next! Although the change in Sarah wasn't a big one at this stage, I knew that every contact my daughter had with the Holy Spirit would bring her closer and closer to God, and change would be inevitable.

The next influence on Sarah, and particularly on Tim, was the movie "The Passion of the Christ" by Mel Gibson. It had come out some months before, and I had a copy at home. We sometimes make the mistake of believing that everyone, whether a Christian or not, must know the story of Christ. This is far from the truth. I invited Tim to watch the movie so he would understand a bit more about why people went to church, and about the Salvation message. I knew salvation was the key for these young people to find release and healing from their drug addiction. It's not enough to get someone off drugs, but the need is to replace the fix with something more meaningful and lasting. What made the Passion movie so powerful was the fact that it graphically showed what Jesus went through to give us the gift of eternal life. The suffering that should have been ours, and which Jesus himself didn't deserve!

One day, Sarah and I had gone out, and we came back to find that Tim had been watching the movie. He was excited to talk about it, and I tried to use every opportunity to talk about the love God had for him. Despite this, Tim would try my patience over and over, and I would wonder if the nightmare would ever end!

A MOVIE, A MAN OF GOD, AND AN EX-DRUG ADDICT

About this time, I was invited to the woman's conference at the Wesleyan Methodist church with my pastor's wife and a few ladies. I was in need of spiritual sustenance, and Christian women's fellowship, to keep me focused on what God was doing. While at the conference, I learned that, in the evening, a young woman named Bronwen Healy would be speaking. I asked someone who she was, and they told me she was an ex-drug addict, and had written a book about how God had healed her of that addiction. I was overwhelmed at the thought that I had two young people at home who needed to hear this woman, but I didn't know how to get them there. It is ironic that often the people who need to hear the testimonies of those who have struggled with life's problems, are the last ones to have the opportunity to hear them. I suddenly thought of my friend, Heather, and rang her.

"Heather, it's Roberta here. I'm at the Wesleyan woman's conference in Brisbane. I have just heard that a young lady, named Bronwen Healy, is speaking tonight about how God set her free from drug addiction. Would it be possible for you to see if Tim and Sarah would come, and would you be willing to bring them?"

I waited for Heather's answer, praying that Sarah and Tim would say yes and, of course, if Heather would be willing to drive from the Sunshine Coast, an hour away, to bring them.

Finally, she said, "Roberta, I would be happy to bring them, and will ask if they'll come with me."

I fervently prayed that Heather could convince Sarah and Tim to come. We had tea at the church, and waited for the moment that Bronwen would give her testimony. I was nervous and agitated as I waited to hear from my friend. Finally, I got the message that Heather was bringing these two young people with her. I was overwhelmed, and excited that they would get to hear, first hand, a testimony of a person's conversion from drug abuse to a new life in Christ.

I sat there with Heather, Sarah, and Tim, and heard Bronwen's story. It was an amazing story and I later bought her book, 'Trophy of Grace'. Sarah would read that book for herself later. As I sat there, I was so grateful to the Lord for orchestrating this opportunity, and so thankful for my friend taking the time to bring these two young people that I could have cried! I looked around me at all the ladies, and thought that they probably didn't need to hear this story as they would have been Christians a long time, and would have heard many similar testimonies but, to these two sitting beside me, it was a miracle! I felt that for those two alone she was speaking! It was another ministry, and another Christian, who was able to speak into my daughter and, if he would listen, to Tim!

Chapter 37

A CHALLENGE FOR 'TEEN CHALLENGE'

I had spoken to Sarah about getting help through Mercy Ministries, and the seed had been planted. The question was what to do about Tim? These two young people seemed to be doing alright but, underneath, I knew there was a long way to go.

Sarah was able to get a casual job at a large farm Expo nearby. Instead of going herself, Tim was determined to go too, and they got in the battered Nissan and left for the Expo. I went out for the day and, as I was driving back home, passed the Nissan, with Tim sitting on the verge near the side of the road! The police had pulled him over, and were examining the car.

Tim was supposed to be with Sarah at the farm Expo, and here he was with the police. I left him to it, and waited for him to get to the house which was only round the corner. I couldn't believe they allowed him to drive the car back! Looking a bit sheepish, he tried to explain that he had become bored at the Expo, and decided to drive home. I don't even think he had a valid driver's license at the time and, as the car was a wreck, of course the police would have their eye on the car!

I was surprised that they had given Tim an ultimatum to get tyres, and a few things done within a month, or the car would be taken off the road. I wondered at the police not finding any drug paraphernalia in the car or, worse, just taking the car off the road there and then. So, of course, my daughter who was at work, needed her mother to then pick her up! At times these multiple inconveniences would drive me to distraction! I would try to put a brave face on things, but each day would continue to bring new challenges.

I would continue to work as a nurse, look after my other three children, and continue the fight for these two, often stubborn, young people. The next day I decided to take Sarah to work myself, and Tim and the boys came too. I made a day of it and decided, after dropping Sarah at work, to spend a few hours at Bribie Island, and have a walk on the beach. I felt it was important to treat Tim as a member of the family and, although he was impulsive and could be very irritating at times, he needed a sense of affirmation. He needed to know he wasn't all bad, and that he could live a better life. He needed to know that God loved him, and cared for him, and was his Father. Tim never knew his real father. He was brought up by his step-dad. I am sure he meant well, but Tim was never going to be good enough. He wasn't given the assurance that he could amount to something. I remember overhearing a conversation with his step-father one day.

"Hi, Dad. It's Tim. Doing okay, just thought I'd let you know that I got a job!"

"Really, Tim. Another job! How long will this one last?"

The look of disappointment on Tim's face just broke my heart, and I looked away not knowing what to say. The sad thing about it was, the job didn't last long, and Tim again took off on another drug binge!

Before this happened, I spoke to a man who ran Teen Challenge up at Nambour. I spoke to him about Tim, and he said he could maybe get him a place at Teen Challenge at Toowoomba. It's a drug rehab centre for men. The problem was, Tim was attached to my daughter, and didn't want to leave her. I also wondered if he was ready to give up his past lifestyle. However, I told Tim that it was an opportunity to get off drugs, and get his life in order. He grudgingly accepted the offer of being driven to Toowoomba, and trying Teen Challenge. I wrote a letter, gave them a donation towards their ministry, and we said goodbye to a reluctant Tim. The kind man from Nambour picked him up, and he said goodbye to Sarah. I will admit to feeling a huge sense of relief, as now I could concentrate on my daughter and getting her the help she required.

Sarah managed to get a waitress job at the Beerwah RSL Club where her ex-boyfriend, Lewis, worked while doing his social work degree at university. I was secretly happy that she was working there, and had contact with Lewis. It was also an opportunity for Sarah to earn money to fix up the car, and to pay many of the debts she had accumulated. But peace and tranquillity were not to last.

I was busy doing my housework one day, only a few days since we had said goodbye to Tim, when I looked up from what I was doing to see Tim looking at me, again with that sheepish little boy look which said, 'Oh dear you're not going to like this'.

"Hi, Mrs Brown. I'm back."

"What are you doing back here, Tim?"

"I couldn't handle people telling me what to do. The other men were very aggressive, and wanted to pick fights with me, and I wasn't even allowed to smoke! I just couldn't take it."

I wasn't all together surprised. He had been brought up with an extremely controlling stepfather, and he just couldn't have people telling him what to do, even when it was for his good. He knew I wasn't happy with his decision, and I tried not to look too disappointed.

Sarah was working, but Tim would just hang around the house. Although I appreciated him helping with the shopping, and fixing a plumbing problem we had, it wasn't helping the household budget. I encouraged him to find a job, and also made it clear that he would have to move out at some time. I was concerned for my other children, and the fact that it was a house which had few rooms. Some of the bedrooms were made up using cupboards and wardrobes! There was essentially no privacy, and only one bathroom for six people. During this time, I tried to encourage Sarah and Tim to go to church, especially if they meant business about changing their lifestyle. They decided to go to the big Outreach centre on the motorway, where Sarah had been prayed for by John Mellor, the healing evangelist. It was the very church that poor Tim had bolted from a few months before. Off they went, and I breathed a huge sigh of relief and prayed that the Holy Spirit would do his work in them. You can imagine my surprise, a few hours later, to see Tim standing in the doorway wrapped in a towel and obviously wet.

"Where have you two been? You told me you were going to church! You weren't meant to go swimming at the beach!"

Tim just grinned, and said, "Guess what I just did?" I nearly had a heart attack when he turned to me and added, "I've just been Baptised!" I could not get over it.

Apparently, Sarah and Tim had arrived at church to find out there was a Baptism service on, and Tim chose to get up on that stage and be Baptised. I do feel it was a gesture which was meant to help him keep Sarah, and be in her mother's good books, but who knows. I would like to think it was a real experience for him. The parable of the sower talks about the seed, which is God's word, falling on different kinds of soil. Some on fertile soil, and others amongst weeds and rocky soil. Unfortunately, I feel it was on rocky soil that the seed fell with Tim, but I still pray for him to this day, and I know he has had a few God encounters along the way.

The message of Salvation is a simple one, and conversion can happen in an instant, but it takes a lifetime to get to know God and to allow him to continually minister to the heart. We can know Christ with the head, but he wants to change our heart, and that is the work of the Holy Spirit. The latter sometimes takes years to work through but, as the verse in Philippians 1:6 says, *"being confident of this very thing, that He who has begun a good work in you will complete it until the day of Jesus Christ."* God is still working it out in each one of us. We are all on a journey of discovering who we are in Christ. No matter who we are, and how much biblical knowledge we possess, we are not done yet! There is much God wants to impart to us, if we are willing to be open to God's Spirit of Truth.

Chapter 38

A BEAUTIFUL GRADUATION AND A HUGE DISAPPOINTMENT

My youngest daughter, Leah, was looking forward to her big day, as she was about to graduate from high school. I took her shopping in Brisbane to find the perfect dress for her. When Sarah graduated, it seemed perfect as she was to graduate with her boyfriend, Lewis, who was school captain, and both were eager to chase their dreams. It wasn't to turn out as they expected after graduation, and much has happened since then.

Leah had her heart set on serving God from the start, and was to enrol in a Bible leadership college, which she would complete in two years, and then study to be a chaplain with Scripture Union. From the age of 15 she worked at Australia Zoo, the home of the famed Crocodile Hunter, Steve Irwin. Leah worked in retail there, and would often catch a glimpse of Steve, Terry, or young Bindi, around the zoo. Leah continued to work there through her studies, and would be working there at the time of Steve's

A BEAUTIFUL GRADUATION AND A HUGE DISAPPOINTMENT

untimely death by the stingray barb. I remember going to the memorial service, as Leah was able to get me a ticket. Leah would be part of the crew ushering people to their seats.

I was being shown my seat, which would be up behind Terry and Robert, and the manager of the zoo, when I saw one of the VIPs waiting to be shown where to go. I looked at this man, who was a few feet away, and thought he looked familiar. He was to read a tribute poem to Steve, and it was the actor David Wenham, who played Faramir in the Lord of the Rings movie franchise.

It was a very moving service, and I remember seeing young Bindi stand up in front of the TV cameras, and the crowd, and give such a clear and moving tribute to her late father, Steve. I don't think there was a dry eye in the place. It was a very emotional service.

Leah finally found the dress for her perfect graduation night, and I looked forward to going and seeing my youngest daughter finally leave school. I would be left with just her twin brothers at high school. It would be three more years before all my children had finished school. I would have children at Beerwah High continuously for seventeen years! My eldest daughter, Naomi, was one of the foundation students when the high school first opened, and would be 'Student of the Year' as there was only one year-level at the time.

I thought it would be good for Sarah to go to Leah's graduation, and she looked beautiful in a black and white dress. Sarah looked so much healthier since being home, and was so different to the pale, thin shadow that she had been when she arrived from Bundaberg. Earlier we had gone with Leah, and some of her friends, to get photos taken of them, all dressed up in their finery. We went to Kings Beach, overlooking the ocean from the cliff top. It was a beautiful place to get photos. The girls had some surfer friends bring their green VW Kombi van, and take them to their graduation ball. I was there to see them dropped off at the Events Centre in Caloundra. I thought it was going to be a perfect evening, celebrating one daughter's graduation with another, a prodigal daughter who had finally come back home.

I sat with Sarah and a friend, while Leah joined her school friends at another table, and tried to enjoy the evening. Sarah had her phone out all night, and was obviously messaging Tim. Then when it came to eat the buffet meal, she picked at the food, which was included in the cost of the expensive ticket. I knew something was going on, and tried to just ignore Sarah and enjoy Leah's night. Each Year 12 class would take their turn to entertain us, and show us the dances they had practised for weeks. It wasn't fun, however, when Sarah told me that Tim was waiting in the car park, and he wanted to take her out. I was not happy and, since my daughter clearly wasn't about to listen to me, I reluctantly let her go. Later, feeling let down, I would say goodbye to Leah as she went off to enjoy her post-graduation party. I drove home, wondering where Sarah and Tim were, and if they were taking drugs again?

Sarah never came home that night, and I got little sleep as I wondered where my daughter was. They had come so far, and I couldn't bear the thought that they were going back to that old lifestyle. Later that morning, Sarah came home, and I had a bad feeling in the pit of my stomach!

"Sarah, where have you been all night? You do realise you ruined your sister's graduation night, maybe not for her, but certainly for me!" I confronted her about Tim and asked, "Have you and Tim been using drugs again?" I knew by the look on her face that she had. I admit I was extremely angry with both of them!

"Sarah, tell Tim I never want to see him again. After everything I have done for him, to take you away from your sister's graduation, and keep you

A BEAUTIFUL GRADUATION AND A HUGE DISAPPOINTMENT

out using drugs! Tell him to come and pick up his stuff. I will put it all down the end of the driveway!"

I carried his things to the bottom of the driveway, and dumped them there so I wouldn't have to see him. Later that day, Lewis would come round to see Sarah, and it was probably just as well he was not aware of the stressful situation which had just transpired!

Over the next few months there would be many ups and downs, and I would feel we were going backwards. But, of course, God knows there was also progress, and everything was leading to a massive change in my daughter's life. Sarah would continue to work at the RSL club, and see Lewis there. However, Tim was still around, and there was very much a co-dependent relationship between them. Tim did get a job up in Yandina, but he needed a car. He decided to ask his step-father if he could get a loan for a car, and he would pay it off when he started work. Obviously, with Tim's drug history, his step-father wasn't foolish enough to hand over $2,000. Fortunately, he wouldn't allow Tim to find a car by himself on the Sunshine Coast, and he had to return to Bundaberg to find one. This was again a relief to me, and I admit I did pray that God would keep him there to allow Sarah to have some breathing space. My prayers were answered when, no sooner had his step-father found a car for Tim, and paid for it, that it broke down! The part needed wasn't easy to find, so Tim had to stay in Bundaberg until it was fixed! God works in strange ways indeed!

Meanwhile, Sarah was seeing Lewis at work, and he would sometimes drop by to talk to her and see the family. Sarah was also still deciding what to do, and was seriously thinking of going to Mercy Ministries. They sent her a CD to listen to, and some books to read which included testimonies of girls who had gone there.

Tim finally returned with a white tray-back truck which his step-father bought for him. He took the job up at Yandina, and rented a caravan up there. His return was troubling, and Sarah was still pulled to be part of his life. This I couldn't understand, but then I had never been addicted to methamphetamines!

Another step forward came when I found out that there was a doctor, who was a Christian, in South Brisbane. This doctor, I was told, had some success treating people addicted to drugs. I thought it was worth the trip to Brisbane, and booked both Tim and Sarah in to see him. I left both Sarah and Tim in the doctor's room, and waited patiently outside. I was expecting, when they came out, that he would have put them on a program, but I was not prepared for what actually happened! In that doctor's office these two young people would be convinced to give their hearts to Christ, and to say the sinner's prayer. The doctor then prayed for them. They would not see him again, and many may be puzzled at this way of treating drug addiction. It was a first step, of many, and it was so important for both of them to acknowledge Christ as their Saviour!

Chapter 39

MERCY AND A GOD OF SECOND CHANCES

Tim and Sarah would continue to see each other, and she often spent time away at Yandina. I am not foolish enough to think they never took drugs again. I just kept praying all the time, and also prayed with Christian friends. Then Sarah fell pregnant. This was the last thing that Sarah needed, or Tim, but I would encourage her to keep the baby, and that I would support her. I know that Tim was very determined to hang on to Sarah, and obviously this was one way which would keep them tied together.

Within weeks Sarah had a miscarriage and she was devastated. No matter the circumstances of the pregnancy, it is still a great loss to the mother and the father. I sat in Emergency with her, and felt her pain as Sarah dealt with the loss of her baby. When Tim rang home to tell them Sarah had miscarried, his step-father told him that Sarah had probably had an abortion to get rid of the baby! You can understand why this young man was so messed up!

I believe Tim saw this as something which could lose him Sarah and, within a few weeks, Sarah was pregnant again! I was not happy about this, as I felt Sarah was so close to deciding to go to Mercy Ministries. I would never encourage Sarah to abort her baby, and tried to support her. I think Sarah felt joy at the prospect of being a mother and, even though it was less than an ideal situation, I felt this baby would help my daughter regain her life, and her walk with God.

Sarah planned to go to Mercy ministries on the Sunshine Coast, and started the application process. I was so relieved and was glad, because of the baby, that Sarah would not be far away. I think that the pain of the miscarriage, and this new pregnancy, did wake Sarah up, and she decided to stop smoking, drinking, and taking any form of drugs. The change in her was becoming more noticeable.

Meanwhile, Tim was not doing so well, and lost his job, just as his step-father predicted. I was determined to see him get help, as there was now a baby on the way. I again discussed the fact that Sarah would be going away for six months, to help her get her life on the right track, and again encouraged him to get help with Teen Challenge. He reluctantly agreed, and I again called the chap from Nambour who took him up to Teen Challenge in Toowoomba, yet again!

Teen Challenge do an amazing job of transforming young men's lives but, unfortunately, the young man needs to really desire change. It is a Christian organisation and they believe from the outset you need to give up any type of drug totally. This includes smoking.

Tim, again, lasted only two days and, instead of coming back to the Sunshine Coast, decided to get a bus to Tamworth in NSW. Who knows what made him do this, but I suspect that he was feeling a little bit guilty at giving in, and may have felt he was letting me down. I was becoming increasingly frustrated with this young man. Tamworth was where he had grown up and, although he could have gone back to Bundaberg, he didn't. Although, in my heart, I felt he was not the right young man for Sarah, nevertheless I continued to pray for him. Later Tim would return from Tamworth, as it was hard to get work there, but he would see God's hand in the experience.

He was later to share with me that he called at the home of an old school friend, and his friend's mother opened the door. She was surprised to see him. This dear lady looked at him, and told him she had just been praying for him. You could imagine her surprise, and his, as they realised how God had brought them together. It was a great encouragement to Tim to show that God was, indeed, real!

It was a very strange tale of three young people, whose lives were tied together. The young woman, who was my daughter, who had been brought up a Christian, had lost her father at a young age, and struggled with life, in the end turning to drugs after meeting another dysfunctional young man. Then there was Lewis, Sarah's high school sweetheart, who had gone overseas for a year, and returned to find the love of his life living a totally different life from the one she had when he left. Sarah had broken off the relationship many months before.

Lewis must have been very hurt, and heartbroken, to think Sarah had seemed to throw away her life, and be with someone so different from himself. I imagine there were many deep emotions that he struggled with as he worked alongside Sarah, and often came over to the house, as a friend, to see how she was going. I believe there was some jealousy there, but Lewis never betrayed his emotions, and always presented a cool exterior to Tim. I remember having a meal with Tim at the RSL club one evening, and Lewis was serving. He went out of his way to be polite, and made sure Tim had a chocolate, even though he hadn't ordered coffee.

I remember another night when I was ordering pizza at a local restaurant. Lewis was at work around the corner at the RSL, and I wasn't sure where Sarah was until I saw her drive past and then Tim, in his car, seeming to chase her. Over the railway tracks they went, and it was like a scene in a movie. I knew where Sarah was going, and it was to see Lewis, and Tim didn't like it. So, of course, I didn't want to see them in trouble, so I jumped in my car to give chase to the other two, and follow them to the club! It's strange what we remember! It was a triangle that I found myself in the middle of. I love my daughter, and very much cared for her ex-boyfriend whom I had always thought to be a special young man. But Tim was a lost young man, and needed help too! The truth of the matter was that the Lord needed to work in all three young people, and that was something I could only pray about.

Meanwhile Sarah had continued with the application process to go to Mercy Ministries. There were two problems that had to be overcome. One was that the house, which was on the Sunshine Coast, closed down almost overnight. It was a shock, as I felt this was so important for Sarah. The other problem was that Sarah was almost three months pregnant, and the Mercy program was for a year! What was to happen now? There were so many ups and downs, and I was becoming weary of it all. Trying to cope with work, and the younger children, and the dramas of my daughter.

The solution presented to Sarah by Mercy was that she would be accepted to the program, but would have to complete it in six months. The other part was that she would have to go to the house in Sydney to do it. When they rang Sarah from Sydney, to offer her the chance to go down there, I was at work and I remember thinking how devastated I was to be told that my daughter would have to go to Sydney! I wanted to nurture her, and her unborn baby, and to have her leave was difficult for me to comprehend! I was glad I was at work, and that Sarah had decided to go to

Sydney by herself, because I knew it was the best thing. I had to let go, and allow God to do what He willed for my daughter and her baby.

Tim was away in Tamworth, and had no say as to what Sarah was going to do. The day came when Sarah was to say goodbye to the family, and Lewis, and I took her to Brisbane airport. It was a tearful, but happy time, as I knew God was going to transform this young woman into someone He could use one day for his glory!

Chapter 40

MERCY AT LAST

Sarah was met at Sydney airport by members of the Mercy team, and was driven to a beautiful big house in Baulkam Hills near the Hillsong Church campus. There she met the staff, and other girls from different backgrounds also struggling with life-controlling issues. The girls lived together, and cooked and cleaned together. They worshipped God every morning, and did their Bible studies. They also worked through the plan that would help change their lives. Learning about what the Bible said about who they were, and how special they were to a loving God, was so important. To understand who Christ is, and how He had a unique plan for each of their lives.

Sarah had a busy time because she had a baby due in six months, and had to work through the program in half the time of the other girls. Sarah was at an advantage because she was from a Christian home, so she was already familiar with the Bible, and much of what it contained. She had given her life to Christ, even throughout the tumultuous years of her life. The girls were encouraged to listen to tapes of well-known Christian speakers. This was to help them change their old mindsets, the negative messages concerning themselves that had bombarded their thinking, and their self-worth. Sarah's favourite was Joyce Meyer, and she would listen to these almost every day. I could tell within a few weeks that my daughter's old life was starting to slip away, and she was being transformed slowly into the person that she was always meant to be.

The staff there were amazing, and Sarah would go for her ante-natal appointments once a month, while someone from Mercy would accompany her. Sarah had a counsellor whom she spoke to regularly and, because Mercy was near Hillsong Church, the girls would worship on a Sunday there, and attend Sisterhood meetings on a Thursday morning. It was great that they could hear wonderful women of God speaking to them, and encouraging them to continue to trust Him. For Sarah it wasn't difficult to join in worship and understand the messages, as she had a Christian background. Sarah was also able to guide some of those girls herself, as she began to share what she had learned with those who were unfamiliar with the Bible. You can imagine how foreign the Christian life was for many from non-Christian homes!

I missed my daughter terribly, and looked forward to our talks on the telephone and her letters. I was allowed to visit Sarah in Sydney, and so one of my eldest daughters, Esther, and I decided to visit her. We booked accommodation near the harbour and King's Cross. Sarah took the train from the Hills, and was able to stay with us for two nights. It was a special time, and we wore poor Sarah out as we walked everywhere, and enjoyed the sights of Sydney, one of the most iconic cities in the world. My daughter was beginning to show her baby bump, and I was excited about this coming grandchild.

I was in awe of how God had gone from bringing my daughter home, to allowing me to hear about Mercy Ministries. It seemed like a lifetime since I first looked up the Mercy Ministries website. I knew that if Sarah could get there, she would receive the help she needed. And now she was actually here, I could already see the impact it was making on her life. The Holy Spirit was working in her to bring her out of darkness!

While Sarah was in Sydney, my brother's family in Perth was going through its own crisis. I found out from my father that one of my nieces had been sick. She was a mother of two girls, and had not been feeling well for some time. Doctor after doctor couldn't find anything wrong until, finally, one took a blood test which showed that she had advanced liver disease from drinking alcohol. She was only 25 years old! We were all in shock! By the time she was in hospital, the doctors gave her only a few weeks to live unless she had a liver transplant. My niece has a rare blood type, and she was critically ill. I encouraged everyone I knew to pray for her, and informed her cousin down in Sydney to pray at Mercy Ministries. Sarah even put an urgent prayer request in at Hillsong Church. Within two weeks, two livers became available, both would be the right blood type. A few days after that and she was recovering from the transplant! I spoke to my niece on the phone.

"How are you doing, Rachel?" I asked.

"So much better, thanks Auntie," Rachel replied.

"Rachel, you know how blessed you are to have come through this!"

"Yes, Auntie. I know! I'm very thankful!"

"God has worked a miracle in providing a liver for you, and bringing you through the operation. Many people around Australia have been praying for you."

"Thank you for your prayers, Auntie, and I do thank God that He has got me through this. Even the surgeon who did the operation could not believe what a miracle it was! He said that God must have been at work because, in all of his forty years of being a surgeon, he had never seen someone get two compatible livers in such a short time!"

While God was saving my daughter, He reached out and also saved her cousin on the other side of Australia!

Chapter 41

A BABY CALLED GRACE

The six months at Mercy Ministries passed quickly, and Sarah's baby was soon due to be delivered. I was looking forward to having Sarah home, and drove out to the airport to meet her. As it happened, Lewis was saying goodbye to his mother at the airport. She was flying up north to stay with her parents. They were also waiting for Sarah as she got off the plane from Sydney.

My daughter looked amazing. Glowing with soon-to-be motherhood, and looking so healthy! Such a different girl from the one whom I begged to come home from Bundaberg, over a year before. I could tell Lewis was pleased to see Sarah too and it was a lovely reunion. We said goodbye to Lewis and his mum and headed home.

It was to be a busy few weeks, as there was to be a new baby in the house. I could see that our current living arrangements were not going to be satisfactory with the addition of a baby, so we needed to move into a larger home. By the time we found a suitable place, Sarah was scheduled to have a C-section the day after our move! It was a huge undertaking, which also meant a large increase in rent. Sarah would help with the rent, as I still had the twins and Leah living with us. Sarah and the baby would have the room with the ensuite, as it was large and big enough for a cot. It would be strange having a newborn in the house again, as my babies (Joe and Ben) were now 15!

I was very grateful to my church at Glasshouse for their help in moving me once again. It is always so stressful a time. We had been in the house in Old Gympie Road for four years. which had been a few years of financial blessing as it was very cheap rent. It was in a nice bush block, but close to town and opposite the boy's primary school. The new house was more modern, and I think that the family very much appreciated the upgrade!

The big move was on the first of October 2008, and the reason the date is so vivid to me is that, the very next day, my beautiful granddaughter, Grace, came into the world! A few weeks before it was discovered that Grace was breach and, although attempts were made to turn the baby, it wasn't to be. Sarah was booked in for a caesarean section, and grandma got to be present at the birth to support my daughter.

This would be only my second grandchild, as my first grandchild, Caleb, was born three years before. I had the privilege of being at my grandson's birth too! This would be different, as it was a caesarean birth and the father wasn't present.

Sarah went through first to have her epidural, and I waited while it took effect. I was then given a cap, gown, and shoe covers to put on, before being ushered into the theatre. This was the first caesarean section I had witnessed. Despite having had eight children, I had never had a caesarean. A large sterile green sheet covered Sarah, and hid the actual operation from view. Sarah was awake, and I was able to sit beside her while the procedure got under way. I was grateful to God for being here with my daughter, and the emotions of seeing my daughter's daughter born, after the nightmare of the last few years, was overwhelming! Suddenly there she was a reddish bundle, with a healthy cry and a good weight.

"Here you are, Grandma. Would you like to be the one to cut the cord?"

"I would be honoured to cut the cord," I replied.

The father usually does this but, of course, the father wasn't present. As much as Tim would have liked to be there, Sarah was against it as they were no longer together. The nurse clamped the cord which was still attached to the placenta, and then handed me surgical scissors to cut the area that was pointed out to me. In all the years of nursing, I had never cut the umbilical cord of a new-born baby!

The nurse said, "You can hold your new granddaughter while your daughter has her stitches!"

They quickly wrapped her up, and the nurse passed the baby to me! I looked in wonder at this beautiful baby, and especially the very beautiful mouth with full red lips!

"Oh, how beautiful she is!" I exclaimed to Sarah.

Grace has the most incredible smile! I cuddled her, and sat with her next to Sarah so she could see her lovely daughter for the first time. I thought of all the hours of prayer and supplication I had made to God for this daughter of mine. The hours of worry, and remembering the many times she could have been snatched away from me because of the scourge of drug addiction. I praised God for His mercy and goodness, especially His Grace on seeing us through one of the worst times of our lives.

I handed Grace to the nurse to have her check-up, as I accompanied Sarah out to the recovery room. As I stood beside Sarah's bed, a friend who was working that shift congratulated Sarah and myself on the birth, and was able to take some photos for me. Grace was born in the hospital where I worked in as an RN for the past five years. It was special seeing my beautiful daughter and granddaughter together, and to see the look of love in my daughter's eyes as she held her new baby girl.

Maybe many of you reading this would think that it was better for this baby to have been aborted, to give my daughter a chance to start her life over, but this was not even considered for one second as two wrongs do not make a right. The life of drug abuse was wrong, and Sarah had to work through so many painful memories, and deal with the underlying issues which lead to the lifestyle she had led. To add to the burden, the guilt of having an abortion would not help the situation. God would use this beautiful baby girl to be a part of my daughter's healing journey. The name, Grace, being fitting for the amazing Grace that God had shown my daughter while she was afar off, and the protection He covered her with until she returned. Grace was the beginning of a new life for Sarah!

If, for any reason, you have had an abortion, God is a forgiving God, and I urge you to talk to a Christian counsellor. There is no need to be burdened with guilt and, if there is repentance, God is a loving, forgiving God, and can help in your loving restoration to Grace. So many young women are convinced they have no choice but abortion, but this is not so. There are many organisations that are there to help if you choose to keep your baby. Mercy Ministries in America help unwed mothers, and support them through pregnancy. They also help place the babies with loving Christian families if the girl, for whatever reason, decides not to keep her baby. So many loving couples would love the chance of becoming parents, but are robbed of the chance because there are so few babies to adopt.

Sarah, baby Grace, and I would go to Sydney once more. This time it would be a celebration of what God had done in my daughter's life. Sarah would go back to the Mercy house and, with baby in arms, would give a powerful testimony of what God had done in bringing her home. Her friend, Lin, who was from Malaysia, would also give her testimony about how she came to go from a high paying job in London, to being desperate enough to fly to Sydney, Australia, to go to a home called 'Mercy'! Some of the Hillsong band were there and, with fervour, we sang the song 'Amazing Grace' by Chris Tomlin – "My chains fell off I've been set free, my God my Saviour has ransomed me!" How amazing is His Grace!

Chapter 42

DANCING AGAIN

Three weeks after Grace was born, Sarah turned twenty. It had been almost three years since she danced, and failed the heartbreaking audition at the Queensland University of Technology. This was mainly because she had no ballet training. Before Grace turned one year old, Sarah had decided to return to dancing. She signed up for classes at the Machaneh Christian School Of Dance at Woombye, to do contemporary, jazz and ballet! While Sarah danced, I would take Grace for a walk around Woombye in her pram.

It was a wonderful dance school. Some of their more seasoned dancers belonged to a group that performed in Israel. The movements of the children were for one thing only, and that was to glorify God! They would lift their hands in worship, which was so different from some of the moves performed by children in other dance schools. Sarah had been dancing for six months, less than a year after her caesarean section, when they had their mid-year concert. The school also had singers perform, and some of the voices were inspiring.

Lewis's mother offered to babysit, and I remember my friend, Heather, and I sitting in the audience with Lewis. This dear lady had spent hours praying for Sarah and myself over the last few years. The moment came when Sarah performed a ballet number, dressed in a beautiful peacock looking outfit with a group of other dancers. As she came on stage, lithe and graceful up on *pointe* dance shoes, Heather and I both started crying. Tears coursed down my face as we watched my 20-year-old daughter dance *en pointe* for the first time ever on stage. This girl, who's dream to be a dancer was shattered three years before, was dancing to the Lord.

She danced a few more dances, and no one watching would believe what she had gone through, especially having given birth to a baby girl just nine months before. I thought how good God was, and what miracles He had performed. One of the highlights for me was the little girls in their pretty tutus coming on stage, with their hands raised in praise and their beautiful, sweet faces lifted to Heaven! The song in my heart was, 'To God be the glory, great things He has done'.

I recalled the words of an ex-dance teacher and adjudicator who told me, years before, that if a young girl didn't start ballet at a very young age, then she would never make a dancer! What is impossible with man, is possible with God!

What worked in Sarah's favour was that she had danced a lot in primary school, doing her lip sync competitions, which was also the start of her gift of choreography. Her dancing and choreography through high school, and her athletic pursuits, all had kept Sarah fit, and had given her a good grounding in dance. Her love of dance was to continue, and she would gradually work through her ballet levels, even while pregnant with her third child at the age of 28!

Chapter 43

TIM

Many may be wondering what happened to Grace's father. There was no intention of shutting Tim out of his daughter's life. Grace was given a photo of her dad, and knew she was special. It was very difficult for Tim to accept that he would not be with Sarah, and Sarah made this decision herself when at Mercy Ministries in Sydney. Sarah believed that it wasn't God's will for her to remain with Tim, despite having his baby. At first he was determined to be at the birth, and told Sarah he would be at the hospital regardless. Sarah had said it was not to be, as they were not together and it wasn't appropriate.

While my daughter was in Sydney, Tim had moved south of Brisbane, and we kept in touch. He really meant to try to change his ways. He rented a room, and got a job at the local abattoir. He told me he had bought a Bible and was reading it. I don't know how much of that was true, as he wanted to hang on to Sarah and also please me. I can appreciate the hurt this young man faced, and I still remember to pray for him as he is my granddaughter's birth father.

At the time of Grace's birth, he was back in Tamworth. A few weeks after Grace was born, he visited his daughter. He was overcome with emotion when he saw her, as any new father would be. The problem was that he was not a reliable young man and, although likeable in many ways, his impulsiveness and dysfunctional background would plague him. He had obviously been using drugs of some sort, and had also bought an expensive used car which he had used to drive from Tamworth to Queensland. I silently thanked God for showing Sarah that he was not for her.

Many times Tim would meet Sarah at a park and see his daughter, but the times got further and further apart. Once he failed to turn up, and his excuse was that he had been drinking and had fallen off the motorbike he was riding. He ended up in prison for accumulated unpaid fines. While he was there, he made contact with the Prison chaplain. In a way I was glad because at least he didn't see Christianity as something to avoid, and I believe even now that God can change this young man's life. Sarah has not had any contact with him for a few years now, although she heard he had a new girlfriend called Sarah, and a baby!

Chapter 44

A RAINBOW AND TWO WEDDINGS

As time went on, Lewis and Sarah began to see more of each other. The day came when Lewis proposed, and they became engaged. They had a wonderful engagement party, with all their friends and family.

Lewis's parents were there and, although they had doubts about the wisdom of Lewis being together with Sarah and her having a baby by someone else, they soon fell in love with baby Grace, and have embraced her as one of their own special grandchildren.

The wedding date was set for the 14th of March 2010. This was just under two years from the time my daughter went to Mercy Ministries in Sydney. What a transformation God had made! There was much to do to get ready for the wedding, and one of the important things to do was choosing Sarah's wedding dress. My daughter and I went on a special shopping day in Brisbane, and went round all the wedding and formal dress shops looking for the perfect dress. No matter what my daughter tried on, she looked beautiful and, being a teary person, I had to control myself a few times as I kept thinking how good my God was, and how He had been with me, and Sarah, over the last few years.

Finally, after trying on plain ones, princess ones, and all manner of styles of wedding dress, my daughter finally decided on one she liked. Sarah looked amazing, and I couldn't wait to see the look on Lewis' face when he would see her on the wedding day! A deposit was paid and the job was done.

Next was discussion over the bridesmaids and their dresses. For the bridesmaids, Sarah had three lovely sisters; her married sisters, Naomi and Esther, and her younger sister, Leah. There was also a special young lady whom Sarah shared her transformation with in Sydney. The same young Malaysian girl who gave her testimony alongside Sarah, who had also been saved by Grace and was on a new journey with Christ. Sarah asked Lin to be a bridesmaid, and she said she would love to be involved.

The bridesmaid's dresses were the next concern, and there was much talk about whether to buy them, or have them made. The girls were similar in height, and slim, so it was decided to shop and see if something could be found off the rack. The wedding was in summer, and on a small beach on the Sunshine Coast. The wedding party would be on a grassy area off the beach with the sea behind them. It was to be a casual wedding, so the dresses were not going to be too formal.

After much searching, we walked into a small fashion store and found a salmon pink dress with one off-shoulder, and one strap-over shoulder. They were knee length and beautiful, and we were able to get four of the same dresses for half the cost of more formal dresses. They went with cream-coloured sandals. Perfect for a beach wedding, and they all looked beautiful.

There was one major hurdle to a perfect wedding, and that was the weather. Because we lived in the sub-tropics, the humidity was high in summer, and so rain was always a possibility. It rained on the lead up to the wedding, and there were a few doubts about having the ceremony outside. The other concern was that the piece of council land the wedding was to be held on had not been mowed and, because of the recent rain, was fairly overgrown. Lewis' father rang the council to let them know they needed it mowed before the wedding, as the grassy area was needed for the wedding party and guests. The alternative was to have it at a nearby church, or at the surf club where the reception was to be held.

We stayed in a hotel in Mooloolaba the night before and both families decided to check out the beach where the wedding was to be held. The grass was mown, which was a good sign, but it was windy and spitting with rain. The Christians in the party had been praying, and I felt in my heart that, as God had come through with everything else, He would make sure the weather was just perfect for the next afternoon. As we stood there, suddenly the Sun came out and a rainbow appeared in the sky right over the spot where the ceremony was to take place. I wanted to shout that, yes, it was to be here. But I also wanted confirmation from others. Then Lewis' father suddenly said, "We should go ahead for tomorrow". So we put our trust in God that the weather would be just right!

The next morning there were a few clouds, but we busied ourselves with the wedding rites of hairdos, makeup, flowers, and dressing up. I had the job of keeping baby Grace entertained and, to be honest, it was an exhausting exercise. But nothing would dull the excitement of seeing my daughter marry her high school sweetheart, and I took it all in stride.

The time came when we drove to Neil Street, (funny, my maiden name is Neil) where the small beach was, with views of cliffs, rocks, and sand. The Sun shone and, although a breeze blew, it kept us cool. My eldest son, Aaron, was the one to walk Sarah down the aisle between the rows of guests, as her father was not there to do it. It is sad to think that my husband, Phil, never got to see any of his children married. I followed with the bridesmaids, and baby Grace.

Pastor Brendan took the ceremony, and that was fitting, as Brendan and my previous pastors, Lionel and Jan, knew only too well the pain, tears, and prayers that had made this day possible. Lionel and Jan were there too, as well as many friends who came to witness the event. It was a beautiful ceremony. The best men and the bridesmaids looked very beachy in their salmon pink shirts and dresses, and off-white sandals and pants. There were family photos, and then the wedding party left to get some shots at various Sunshine Coast locations. God's presence was there, and it was just such a joy to witness!

As we enjoyed the reception at the local surf club, overlooking the beach, the weather suddenly turned. The staff at the surf club had to hurriedly lower the blinds on the verandah to stop the rain coming in. How amazing is our God, providing a beautiful afternoon despite the unpredictable weather!

At the reception there was much joy as we celebrated the union of Lewis and Sarah. There was great food, dancing and, of course, speeches! My father gave a speech, and also Lewis' grandfather, where they honoured the Lord and His goodness!

It also took me back two years to another wedding. The wedding of my son, Jacob, to his childhood sweetheart, Alex. At the time Jacob got married, Sarah was on her journey home to the Lord. It would have been about the time she first fell pregnant with Grace. There was still so much uncertainty for my daughter's future. That is why it is so important to look, with spiritual eyes, at a situation and not the natural eyes. So many times I could have given up praying and pressing in, so many times in the journey I could have just got on with living, and allowed my despair to rule my life and cause me to give up. The transformation of Sarah from the time of her brother's wedding to her own was astounding, and many might think that she would have come good, even without prayer. I agree there are instances where people, who are addicted to drugs, can make a recovery, but it is extremely difficult, and often the drug addiction is replaced with another addiction. It requires a complete transformation of the mind. The realisation that, despite failures and addiction, God still loves you, and is willing to redeem you through His blood. The drug addict also needs the motivation to change, and this can be difficult. I feel that strategic prayers are so important to help loosen the grip of the enemy. They can loosen the hold of the addiction over the person.

Just to have Sarah present at Jacob's wedding, was a small victory. All along the journey there were small victories to be celebrated. Jacob and Alexandra's wedding was on the Blackhall Range up at Maleny, looking over the beautiful Glasshouse Mountains. It was a beautiful day, and a wonderful reception. My daughter-in-law once told the music teacher at high school, soon after she and Jacob had started dating, that he would play at their wedding one day. My son played the saxophone at school, and his teacher was in the Royal Australian Navy Band. Four years later, and there he was playing his trumpet as Alex walked down the aisle!

A special thing that happened, captured on the video, was that a butterfly was flying around them and, as they began saying their vows, the butterfly landed on Alex's dress. Alex and Jacob's minister took the ceremony. They have lived in London, and now live in New York where Jacob is a civil engineer, and Alex works for an advertising company. Working in London gave Jacob a lot of experience in urban planning in a big city and, by the time Jacob and Alex went to New York, he was ready to tackle the Big Apple! The engineering firm he worked for were given the opportunity to build the new 911 memorial, which is a memorial walk through an avenue of huge stone slabs, with metal from the twin towers entwined in between them. This part of the 911 memorial was to remind people of the many who died since 911, from the toxins and injuries that were sustained when the twin towers fell. These included civilians, rescue workers, and firemen. What a privilege to have my son involved in this huge project. I have seen the memorial first hand, and the site makes you wonder how it would have looked when the twin towers collapsed! They have now welcomed twin girls into the family, born in Brooklyn, and I couldn't be happier for them! Before they got married, they had been living and studying for their degrees in Toowoomba, over 130 kilometres west of Brisbane.

At the time, Sarah was struggling, and had just come home. We had all gone up to Toowoomba for the annual Easterfest. This was a celebration of Easter, put on by the combined efforts of the Toowoomba churches. An amazing experience of Christians coming together from all around Australia to hear Christian bands, fellowship, worship God, and enjoy being together in an awesome part of Queensland. The highlight of many of these times was when there was a combined church service in Queen's Park, and we would worship our wonderful Saviour under the stars together.

One time I remember standing beside my youngest son, Ben, as we sang 'How Great Thou Art'. Hearing him sing was such a blessing to me. It was while waiting for the combined church service, under the big top, on Easter Sunday morning, that I had been praying that Sarah and Tim would come to the service. It was with gratefulness that I saw them enter the big top and join us. Every occasion that brought them closer to God, and brought them under the working of the Holy Spirit, was another victory!

Sarah and Lewis' wedding reception ended after much cool dancing from everyone, including my much-loved parents, and my grandson, Caleb, who just killed it on the dance floor! It was a very big night for one young girl, and I headed off early to put young Grace to bed, and also to put to bed one very tired grandma!

The next morning a few of the family members had breakfast together, and then Lewis' parents took baby Grace home for a few days, as Lewis and Sarah embarked on their honeymoon on an island in the Whitsundays. I then looked after Grace for a few days before they returned.

The honeymoon was not without its dramas, as there was a cyclone off the Queensland coast and, during one of the nights there, all the guests had to sleep in the lounge room of the resort. At least Sarah and Lewis were a few days into their honeymoon, but another couple had to literally spend the very first night of their honeymoon with a room full of strangers!

Chapter 45

TWO NEW GRANDSONS AND A FLOOD!

As Sarah and Lewis began their new life together, Lewis continued with his social work, and Sarah did jobs like house cleaning and ironing, as well as selling Amway for a while. Throughout these years my daughter continued to attend her dance classes, and continued to train as a dance teacher. They also added to their family when baby Izaac was born in January 2011, only 10 months after their wedding.

The week of Izaac's birth was one not soon forgotten. Three of my daughters, and their families, would be affected by a major catastrophe in South East Queensland. A major flood would devastate parts of Brisbane, Toowoomba, Ipswich, and even affect parts of the Sunshine Coast. The last major flood to affect Brisbane was back in 1974!

Two daughters were due to give birth in the first month of 2011. Another daughter was also undergoing fertility treatment.

I haven't been present at all my grandchildren's births and, of course, it is up to my children and their spouse's wishes. The births I have had the privilege of attending have been very special for me. Every birth of a grandchild, whether I am there or not, is a wonderful blessing from God, and I am so grateful for each one of them! Sarah and Lewis allowed me the privilege of being present at baby Izaac's birth. Lewis' parents, Alf and Janet, looked after Grace when Sarah went into labour. Sarah had Grace by planned C-section because she was breech. Because Sarah was young and fit, they allowed what is called 'a trial of labour', where they allow the mother to continue in labour as normal unless it stops progressing, then they would do another C-section.

I had prayed Sarah would be able to have a normal birth, and everything seemed to progress well. To give Sarah a rest from her contractions they had given her an injection, which gave her a chance to sleep and save her strength. The midwife had come to check if my daughter was dilating sufficiently to continue in labour or, if there were not sufficient signs of progression, she would be taken to theatre for another C-section.

Although the midwife was concerned that there was little progression, I felt in my spirit that Sarah was ready to give birth, and I didn't want them rushing to do another caesarean. I prayed fervently to the Lord as they got her ready for theatre. Part of getting her ready was to put an indwelling catheter in her bladder. While they were inserting the catheter, I believe God intervened. She suddenly dilated, and Izaac's head crowned. Everything suddenly changed and, within minutes, my new beautiful grandson was born! One of the nurses was a male nurse who had done his midwifery training, and who had worked with me in the medical ward.

Lewis and Sarah brought Izaac home from the hospital, and then the rains came. Their unit was near Coochin Creek, which started overflowing its banks, and all-over South East Queensland it rained and rained! Lewis rushed over to Caloundra to get sandbags, putting them at the entrance to the units where they lived. Sarah came to stay with me overnight in case

TWO NEW GRANDSONS AND A FLOOD!

the water came over the threshold of their unit. It was special having a new baby in the house again.

Meanwhile in Ipswich, another daughter, Naomi, went into labour, and brought her beautiful boy home the next day, just to be told that the water would soon be in their house. This time the floods came with a vengeance, and my son-in-law, Ben, had to evacuate the family. This was just two days after Sarah stayed with me with baby Izaac and daughter Grace. Naomi came for a couple of nights with young Caleb, Hannah, and new baby Ezra!

Although the waters receded, and didn't affect Sarah and Lewis much, for Naomi and Ben it was far more devastating! They owned their home, and everything that couldn't be moved was destroyed. The damage had come half way up the walls. Queensland has very high humidity at this time of year and, if anything is damp, it turns mouldy. This is very unhealthy to live with. There was no way they could stay there! They were so blessed to have a couple they knew allow them to stay in a unit they were renovating, and it would be their new home for the next three months.

Daughter number three, Esther, and her husband, Richard, had just moved into a rental house in Chelmer, a suburb of Brisbane. They had been living for a few years in a flat in Taringa, which was nowhere near the flooding Brisbane River! Esther and Richard were unaware of the imminent threat until some very good friends turned up with some trailers, and urged them to pack up the house before the floods came. Already feeling overwhelmed from continued fertility treatment, and the cost of this on her mental health, Esther struggled coping with, again, having to live in a Toowong unit block, surrounded by university students!

Many suburbs of Brisbane were affected that year. Lives were lost, and millions of dollars' worth of damage were afflicted on many communities. Queensland is not a stranger to disasters and, as a young family, we even went through a cyclone up in the north of the state. But what is utterly amazing about these disasters is that people come together like never before, and we reminded ourselves that we were created by God to live in community, and to love one another in practical and supportive ways.

Not only did the State Emergency Services get called into action, but neighbourhoods came together to clean the mud from people's homes, to stand side by side in the hot humid, stinking conditions, and work to help restore people's lives! My own small church in Glasshouse took a trailer and some tools, and went into Brisbane to lend a hand. Naomi and Ben's house was completely rebuilt inside, and a church miles away on the Sunshine Coast helped rebuild it. The insurance helped pay for the materials, but much of the work was done by these dear souls. They took time out of their own busy lives to help rebuild the lives of people they didn't even know! Not only did this church rebuild their home, but they paid for a holiday for one week for Naomi's family, and for another family also affected by the floods. I love this verse from Ephesians 2:10 which says, *"For we are His workmanship, created in Christ Jesus for good works, which God prepared beforehand that we should walk in them."*

Soon after this flood, Esther fell pregnant through IVF, and delivered a beautiful baby in December the same year. His name is Theodore. It comes from the Greek 'Theodoros' ('Theos' meaning god, and 'doron' meaning gift). Therefore God's gift! What a gift it was that I had three beautiful grandsons born in 2011 – out of the floods came life in abundance!

Chapter 46

A DANCE SCHOOL IS BORN

In a hall at the local Baptist church in Beerwah, Queensland, in 2015, a dance school was born. In reality it was born in the heart of a young girl of eight when she entered her first lip sync competition at her primary school. A seed was planted that gave her a love of dance, and a gift of choreography. A small spark that helped ignite a dream.

It began small, and with just a few students. The very professional sign that stood outside said 'Masterpiece Dance', with the picture of a colourful dancer on the front. With the skills from Machenah for teaching, and the experience of her dancing through high school, Sarah began her dance school. Teaching hip hop, contemporary dance, and ballet. Ballet was something she thought she could never do, as she started at the age of 20, but was now able to teach to a younger, very enthusiastic generation. My daughter's great love is contemporary dance, and this shows in some of the amazing choreographed dances that are now winning competitions performed by her dancers at Eisteddfods around Queensland.

A few years before, Sarah attended a conference called 'Living the Dream', with an ex-pastor and business man. There were many amazing speakers who inspired others to chase their dreams, and had incredible stories to share. Sarah and Leah were to meet someone who particularly inspired them, especially Sarah. His name is Li Cunxin, and he became the Director of the Queensland Ballet company. He had grown up in China, under communist rule, and his life was the basis of the film 'Mao's Last Dancer'.

"Mr Li. Could my sister and I have a photo with you, please?" asked Sarah. "I love dance and hope to begin my own dance school one day."

"It would be my pleasure, Sarah," said Li.

Sarah and Leah had someone take their photo with the world-famous dancer and choreographer, who married an Australian dancer, and who found a new home here in Queensland. This was a special moment for Sarah, inspired to go for that dream and make it happen!

In the same year she started her dance school, three things happened which helped in the promotion of her school. The school was invited to perform at the annual Beerwah Street Party. It was great to see the little ones dressed up in their colourful costumes, waiting to go on stage. They were so excited, and the routines were wonderful.

The other thing to hold Beerwah residents enthralled, was the fact that their very own Bindi Irwin, Steve Irwin's daughter, had made the final of 'Dancing with the Stars' in America. One of the local councillors had seen Sarah's dancers perform at the street party, and also knew Sarah as she had been School Captain at his son's primary school. He had an idea to send a video to Bindi in America, to show that the local community were behind her. People may never have heard of Beerwah before, but may have heard of Australia Zoo which was home to the Crocodile Hunter, Steve Irwin, who died in 2006 from a stingray barb. Terri Irwin, her daughter Bindi, and son Robert, continue to run the iconic zoo. Australia Zoo is just outside of the township of Beerwah.

A DANCE SCHOOL IS BORN

Sarah's dancers, and a dance troupe from the local high school, choreographed some dances, and locals gathered with placards wishing Bindi well in her competition. It was decided that Sarah would be the spokesperson on the video to be sent to America. She did an amazing job, and had everyone cheer for their local girl, Bindi. My granddaughter, Grace, with her incredible smile, featured a few times in the video!

The third opportunity came at the end of the year, at a carol service performed at the local sport's ground where, again, Masterpiece Dance along with another dance school, were featured. Because Sarah is a Christian, she was able to aim the dances, music, and choreography at promoting the birth of her Saviour, Jesus. The local churches organise and put on the carol service, and it is an amazing night with a combined church's choir singing carols, the presentation of the birth of Christ, and finishing with a mandatory fireworks' display! Not only were the young dancers beautiful, but Sarah herself, with another ballet dancer, performed to the song 'Joyful Joyful'!

Chapter 47

A DANCE SCHOOL FLOURISHES

The dance school began to grow. It was necessary to put on more classes, and hire teachers, as Sarah could not cope on her own. Lewis attended to much of the business side of things, and Sarah is constantly using her creative skills to improve the dance school's curriculum. As well as dance, Sarah felt to include an acrobatics class, as there are often acrobatic elements in modern dance. An acrobatics teacher was hired, and the children love the chance to tumble and do cartwheels and handstands! This meant using two different venues.

Suddenly, Sarah was told that the Christian school at the Baptist church no longer wanted Masterpiece Dance to use their hall and dance studio. This was a big blow, as the church and school, were in a central position, and had areas where parents could wait with younger children. I am sure it was a difficult decision for the church and school, as they needed the facilities for their own growth and use! So, at the end of 2017, Masterpiece Dance needed to find another venue. With nowhere suitable to go, the dance school sought other solutions. Much prayer was made to find a place for Masterpiece Dance which, by now, had over 200 students!

During the school holidays, Sarah and Lewis decided to approach the local real estate about leasing three shops. They were next to each other in a small shopping precinct in Beerwah. It was an area where, apart from a bakery, Post Office, charity shop, and takeaway, there was not much else happening. The shops in question had been empty for some time, and so a deal was struck and Masterpiece Dance now had the huge job of converting three shops into two dance studios, complete with flooring, mirrors, and bars for ballet! With help from friends and family, the transformation took place, finishing just in time for the new school year starting in 2018.

The new venue is central to the schools in the area, and also close to shops so parents can go shopping, have a coffee, or even take their younger children to the nearby Turner Park for a play! There is also plenty of parking! God is indeed good in supplying their needs, and it has been a blessing, as now equipment can stay at the venue, and it is even big enough for the acrobatics mat to be stretched out fully. It also means they can use their own space whenever they want, and can include extra activities; such as a dance party at the end of school term, and extra classes for those doing Eisteddfods.

It took a lot of faith to step out and undertake this massive move, but it has certainly paid off! Recently, because of the growing numbers, the dance school has added a third studio at a nearby hall. My daughter now has four children, a business, and is adding to her school many talented new teachers! God has indeed been good, and I praise Him every single day for what He has done, and continues to do in the family.

Chapter 48

GOD'S GOODNESS ASTOUNDS ME!

As I look back on the many years since my husband died, I wonder how I survived the trauma of losing him, and survived the ups and downs of being sole parent to eight children. When I tell people I have eight children, and 16 grandchildren, with perhaps more in the future, I feel they don't quite believe me. But then I find it hard to believe too! As I have said before, each child we had is a gift from God, and my husband and I desired that, in their own way, we hoped each would choose to serve God. Therefore they are really not our children but His, and it is a privilege partnering with God in seeing them go into the world, and make an impact in whatever endeavours they are led to.

In 2016 I was at a healing seminar for three weeks in beautiful Scotland. The lecturer had us close our eyes and hold out our hands, as she was going to give us a gift. As I had my eyes closed, I suddenly had a vision of a field of wheat and, in the field, a man was walking. I then joined the man, walking through the field. Then a few more people joined us, and a few more, until there were hundreds of people walking behind us through the field. I felt the Lord say that this was our legacy in the Lord. My husband and I, with our eight children, were joined by grandchildren, then great grandchildren, until there was a multitude of people in the wheat field, and we were all walking towards the light of God's glory!

Some of my favourite verses are Psalm 127:3-5 which says:

> *Behold, children are a heritage from the Lord,*
> *The fruit of the womb is a reward.*
> *Like arrows in the hand of a warrior,*
> *so are the children of one's youth.*
> *Happy is the man who has his quiver*
> *full of them; They shall not be ashamed,*
> *But shall speak with their enemies in the gate.*

These verses remind us how precious our children are, and that God blesses those who bring our children to Him. People often speak of having an inheritance and, in this day and age, it is often to do with wealth, land, and material possessions. It is not a bad thing to leave a material inheritance for our children, but often this inheritance is wasted and misused. It is better to leave an inheritance that will last, and invest into our children a love of the Lord and a desire to serve Him. A spiritual inheritance is more important than material goods.

A scripture from Isaiah reads:

> *As for Me, says the Lord, this is My covenant with them:*
> *My Spirit, who is upon you, and My*
> *words which I have put in your mouth, shall not*
> *depart from your mouth, nor from the mouth*
> *of your descendants, says the Lord, from this*
> *time and forever more.* (Isaiah 59: 21)

It promises a spiritual inheritance will be passed onto our children, but we must do our part. It is not an easy job, and there are many pitfalls, but the Lord gives us wisdom and help along the way when we turn to Him and His word for help. Proverbs 3:5 tells us to, *"Trust in the Lord with all your heart, and lean not on your own understanding."*

In Psalm 37:3 it commands us to, *"Trust in the Lord, and do good; dwell in the land, and feed on His faithfulness."*

Life is difficult and, if anyone can say their life is perfect, then I would doubt his words. Difficult times will come to us all. How do we respond to challenges? This simple verse from the Psalms tells us:

To trust in the Lord – Remember He is in control!
Do good - Even when things aren't going well, continue to do what is good despite how others may react to their circumstances.
Live in the land – Live your life, continue to move forward.
Feed on His faithfulness - I believe here the Psalmist is telling us to remind ourselves how faithful God has been in the past. He is Faithful. Remember when he brought you through this crisis, or when you thought it was too much to bear, He helped you get through! Feed on that! We are so good at forgetting God's faithfulness. Like the children of Israel who quickly forgot what the Lord did through Moses in Egypt. Each time there was a crisis they grumbled! Instead, they should have reminded themselves about what God had done for them in the past. We are like those Israelites, quickly forgetting what God has done in the past, or forgetting the promises He has made.

With the chaos in the world today, and the evil that abounds, we need more than ever to feed on His faithfulness! He is in control, even when we can't see what He is doing. When Sarah was in Bundaberg, I could not see what was happening. I could only imagine what was happening. This, of course, only instils fear and a lack of faith. I had to continue to, *"Trust in the Lord, and do good; dwell in the land* (keep on living), *and feed on His faithfulness."* Even when I couldn't see with my natural eyes!

God hears our prayers, but He needs us to, *"Trust also in Him, and He will bring it to pass."* (Psalm 37:5)

To contact the author please email deborahrising@outlook.com

www.ingramcontent.com/pod-product-compliance
Lightning Source LLC
Chambersburg PA
CBHW032108090426
42743CB00007B/282